Flavours of Babylon

With Best wishes,

Linda Dangoor

For my family and
in honour of my parents,
Claire and Abdulla

Linda Dangoor

Flavours of Babylon

A family cookbook

WP

Waterpoint Press

First published in 2011 by Waterpoint Press
Waterpoint Press is an imprint of Romaflow Ltd
48 Sloane Square London SW1W 8AT

ISBN 978 0 9567325 07

A CIP catalogue record for this book is
available from the British Library.

Typography Blacker Design
Design Linda Dangoor & Blacker Design

Printed by Latitude Press

Contents

Introduction

Thanks to its important geographical position, Mesopotamia (present day Iraq) found itself at the crossroads of the trading route for almost two thousand years. As a result, it acquired new spices and products from far away countries such as India and China and came in contact with the culinary traditions of its close neighbours. More recently, the very long Ottoman rule of almost four hundred years (from 1534 till 1918) left an undeniable imprint and helped to enrich its, otherwise simple, cuisine.

Iraqi food is aromatic, robust and spicy – but it is not hot. Herbs and spices such as parsley, mint and coriander; cumin, cinnamon and cardamom; pepper, paprika and saffron are all used extensively – but not chillies. Dates, tamarind and dried limes are favoured for sweet and sour dishes. Almonds and pistachios are included in most desserts and sweetmeats which are invariably perfumed with orange blossom or rose water.

All Iraqis, whether Moslems, Christians or Jews, ate more or less the same food. Their meals consisted, usually, of bread, rice and some kind of vegetable or meat stew. Some communities had religious restrictions in regards to food and this affected the choice of ingredients and the way a dish was prepared. For example, both Moslems and Jews are forbidden to eat pork whereas Christians are not; Jews do not mix dairy products with meat whilst Christians and Moslems have dishes where meat is cooked in a yoghurt sauce or with butter. Both the Jewish and Moslem communities adhere to strict methods of animal slaughter to make their meat kosher or halal, that is to say, fit for consumption. These different communities brought subtle and creative changes, diversifying the culinary tradition of Iraq. Added to this, geographical influences played their part too; communities in the north of the country eat more wheat than rice and their food is closer to the Kurdish and Turkish tradition. On the other hand, the staple food of those further south is rice and, in and around Basra, dishes have a definite Persian touch.

The first recorded recipes were discovered incised on clay tablets in Mesopotamia around 3000 BCE. Recipes were not usually recorded and writings on the subject were uncommon; apart from a few well known cookery manuals compiled during the Middle ages, such as Al-Waraq's Kitab al Tabikh or that written two hundred years later by Muhammad al Baghdadi, serious recordings on the subject were few and far between. Culinary customs and recipes were traditionally a family affair, transmitted orally through the ages, from mother to daughter and from one generation to the next. There could be many variations of a dish because each family would necessarily bring its personal touch, adding more garlic, using coriander instead of mint, date syrup instead of fruit, oil instead of butter, and so on – albeit following the same recipes.

This book does not pretend to be a comprehensive study of Iraqi food, rather, it is a personal collection of my favourite family recipes handed down from one generation to the next; dishes that my grandmothers cooked for us in Baghdad and which my mother and many relatives continue to serve today in London.

In addition, I have also included other recipes inspired by my travels and Middle Eastern background. Putting the two types of food side by side in the same book seems very natural to me. It is the way I cook on a daily basis and it epitomises who and what I am – a mixture of East and West – the result of moving countries many times and of settling in a country very different from my own.

Like so many, I cook intuitively. That is to say, I add a dash of this and pinch of that and adjust the taste as I go along. For this project, however, I made a supreme effort to be meticulous about recording the precise quantities used in each recipe. That said, I encourage you to adjust the seasoning to your liking, as taste is very subjective and the quality of ingredients varies from season to season and country to country.

Talking of taste someone once, asked me what made a dish flavoursome, was it just seasoning? An interesting question certainly, and seasoning does make a difference, but there are many decisions that one has to take that go into making a delicious meal.

Firstly, the **ingredients** you choose will determine the end result, as these are the building blocks of any dish. They should be very fresh and, if possible, in season and organic. Secondly, the **method of cooking**, whether it be baking, grilling, boiling or steaming will determine how the dish will taste. For example, boiling vegetables produces a very bland dish and reduces their nutritional value. Whereas steaming or stir-frying them not only helps to conserve their minerals and vitamins but also produces a delicious dish with the help of a little lemon juice, a drizzle of olive oil and a pinch of cayenne pepper.

Flavour also depends on the **length of time** you cook something; undercooked or overcooked, the dish will vary in taste.

Now we come to the **seasoning**. The quantity of herbs, spices, salt or sugar is crucial as they determine the overall 'perfume' of the dish. I always say taste matters but not at the expense of health or the integrity of the ingredients.

Lastly, the **visual presentation** of a dish plays its part in making it appetising.

Having said that, the most important ingredient, to my mind, is **love**. A meal cooked with love tastes that much better.

A house on the Tigris

My parents, my two brothers and I lived in a house on the bank of the River Tigris with my paternal grandparents, three aunts, three uncles, one grand uncle and four cousins. It was a busy house full of life.

We had a cook called Gershone who catered for the whole household. Nana, our paternal grandmother, decided the fare for the day, supervised the cooking but did not cook herself. Sometimes my mother would venture into the kitchen to make a jam or to bake a few cakes but she never cooked a meal either. Her mother, whom we called Maman, enjoyed food and was a great cook. I remember how flavoursome and aromatic her dishes were.

Maman's chicken rice was superb. The rice was so carefully cleaned before it was cooked that no trace of grit was left in it. This was not always the case with our cook who was not as meticulous; eating his rice was like walking on a minefield, not knowing when our teeth would encounter the next bit of grit, and because we had rice at every meal there was no escape except on the days we went to Mamam.

We had a garden where we played with our cousins, inventing all sorts of games. We had the river for swimming, the sun to bless our days and the stars to lighten up the ink blue night sky. We had fresh bread, baked in our mud oven, situated at the back of the house. We had pomelo trees, fig trees, sour orange and sweet lemon trees,

berry trees and one *nabug* tree (a kind of berry resembling a cherry). During the long summers, all of us slept on the roof at night, as did all Baghdad. We would fall asleep hypnotised by the bejewelled sky.

We had simple and uncomplicated pleasures. We would stick our faces in bunches of jasmine or orange blossom and inhale their sweet fragrance. We ate crisp lettuce to quench our thirst, bit into ripe fruit that tasted better than a sweet, drank cool and delicious water from special terracotta jars – and I have not tasted such delicious water since. We had rosewater sherbet drinks to cool us down in the summer, and hot *shorba* (a kind of thick soup) whenever we had a cold. The summers were sizzling hot in Baghdad, so hot that my skin used to crawl and prickle even when I was indoors. We didn't have air conditioning but we had an ingenious air-cooling system.

These were boxes, made of sheets of trellis cut to the size of the windows, stuffed with clumps of wild thorns and secured to the metal grilles on the outside of the windows (from afar, they looked like thick green mattresses). The whole construction would be drenched in water, trickling from a rubber hose with holes cut along its length, placed at the top of the frame. The hot breeze blowing into the house would be chilled as it passed through the layers of damp thorns and a fresh leafy scent would perfume the air of the rooms. These thorn boxes also served as curtains or blinds to shield the rooms from direct sunlight.

We woke up early with the rising sun and the insistent call of the rooster. Our grandfather woke at the same time and was taken to the market by his driver to do the daily food shopping for the whole household, before going to work. In summer, before breakfast, my father would take my brother, Eddie, and I (Alfred, was too young at the time) for a fast walk along the river to where the women were selling some freshly made qeimar (a glorious version of clotted cream, freshly made from buffalo milk). At the sight of the wooden trays displaying the slabs of cream, thick as butter, our mouths would begin to water. I remember how impatient we all were to return home to sample some. The qeimar was a heavenly start to our breakfast. We spread it thickly on bread, drizzled some date syrup over it and devoured it with gusto, savouring every mouthful with pleasurable mmms and more mmmms.

After breakfast we went to school and returned home to a copious lunch. And while the whole household took its habitual siesta, the jasmine and the orange blossoms perfumed the afternoon air, the river twinkled pink and silver under the setting sun, and the fruits in our garden hung lazily on the trees.

At sunset we went, sometimes, to the river where we would signal to one of the boatmen to give us a ride in his rowing boat. The whole family, my parents, my brothers and I, would squeeze into this narrow *balam* (a small rowing boat). All would be quiet except for the sound of the oars dipping in and out of the shimmering water. After thirty minutes of this gentle promenade, the *balamchi* (boatman) would drop us on the riverbank opposite our front door.

In summer, because of the low tide, small sandy islands would appear in the middle of the Tigris.

These were very beautiful and they transformed the river into a sort of patchwork of earth and water. We call these islands *jezra*. As soon as the weather started to get hot these *jezra* took on the appearance of a camping site. People erected their tents and came to live there during the whole summer because it was cooler and fresher at night. They would go to work in the morning as usual, by catching a rowing boat which dropped them on the river bank.

We were always excited at the sight of these islands. A whole group of family friends would get together to organise our outings. We would clamber into numerous rowing boats, laden with all sorts of food and refreshments for a lazy picnic. There would be meat, fish, hot bread, some vegetables and fruits and various drinks. We made sand castles whilst the adults organised the cooking, and we invariably ate barbecued meat or the *Masgouf* fish (a barbecued white fish) for which Baghdad is famous.

I was ten years old when we left Baghdad for good. We went to Beirut, where we lived for two years in an apartment by the sea. We had a cook called Marie, a Maronite Christian from near Tripoli. My mother organised and guided Marie but did not cook herself. She always accompanied Marie to the abundant and colourful market. There they selected the best fruits and vegetables and the two of them would come back laden with the freshest and tastiest of products.

It was in Beirut that our taste buds were truly awakened. The food was slightly different and more varied than ours and the mezze, that colourful array of small dishes packed with exciting flavours, was a delightful discovery. My brothers and I were very happy living in Lebanon, but there were many things that we began to miss. We missed our *Khoubez*, the Iraqi flat bread, and our Baghdadi water which had an exquisite taste, unequalled anywhere in the world. We missed our grandparents and our Aunt Eileen, who would join us in London fourteen years later, once they were given permission to travel. We missed our school friends, our cook, Gershone, our garden, our river and sleeping on the roof.

It was our first taste of exile.

Cooking with my mother

Tell me and I'll forget, show me and I may remember, involve me and I'll understand.
Chinese proverb

It was when we came to London in the 1960s that my mother's cooking experience began in earnest.

From the beginning she involved me in the kitchen. Leafing through recipes, neatly handwritten by her in an old exercise book, she would choose our Sunday lunch menu and we would start preparing. I washed vegetables; helped her chop enormous amounts of mint and flat parsley for the tabbouleh salad; beat the whites of eggs manually (for what seemed to me to be an eternity) to make mayonnaise; peeled potatoes, grated carrots, squeezed lemons, rolled out pastry to make sambouseks; learned how to kosher the meat by salting it – salt draws out the blood and impurities from the meat, she once told me – and watched carefully as she cooked. I enjoyed being her young sous-chef and it was during these early years that I began to have a good grounding in cooking. I have to confess though, not all our dishes were a great success at first. For one thing we couldn't buy Middle Eastern ingredients in those days. Only a handful of Indian and Greek Cypriot shops stocked those so-called exotic products. But we soon got the hang of it and this learning process quickly involved my brothers too. As a result the whole family cooks today.

My parents entertained frequently in those days. Their parties always consisted of at least 20 to 30 guests. They were grand affairs by western standards with lots and lots of food, the norm for people from the Middle East; hospitality is in our blood and our tables are always generous and elaborate.

Offering food is a pleasure for us. It is the way we honour our guests, a gift that we give to them and to our loved ones.

Although we left Iraq when I was only ten years old, the link to my roots has always been very strong, having retained a sensual connection to the land of my ancestors through food and family gatherings, through language and music.

So the idea for this book developed naturally out of a desire to teach my nephews and the sons and daughters of their generation how to cook the Iraqi dishes they loved so much and, in doing so, pass on some of the heritage of the Babylonian Jews[1] of which they knew very little.

I began by writing down a few recipes with the intention of organising some cooking sessions for my two nephews, Jesse and Reuben, at a later date. Many months passed and my recipe collection had, by now, multiplied ten-fold. Initially, I had assumed that recording our Baghdadi dishes would be an easy and swift affair; a cataloguing job so to speak and that would be the end of the project. Instead, I became so immersed in the subject that it steered me towards something altogether more instructive and fulfilling.

As well as reading various cookery books and those on nutrition or on the history of food, I began taking photographs of all the dishes. I would cook in the morning, check to see if the recipes needed adjusting, then take numerous shots of what I had cooked. After which, I would sit at my computer, type the recipes and

proceeded to design the layout of the book. The work of writing, cooking, photographing and designing spanned over 2 years. During which time, I had the privilege of taking advice from my mother, my two aunts, and many other wonderful women of our Iraqi community who generously shared with me their recipes and their knowledge. We spent very enjoyable moments, chatting and laughing and finally eating whatever we had cooked.

With this book, I hope the discovery of new dishes and exciting flavours will inspire you to cook, eat and feast with pleasure.

Enjoy and Awafi![2]

1. *It is not common knowledge that the Babylonian Jews have lived in Mesopotamia (modern day Iraq) since 530 BCE. Descendants of the tribe of Abraham (who was born in Ur, in southern Iraq), sadly only a few remain in Baghdad today.*

Suffice it to say that mistreatment and persecution over the years have driven this indigenous community out of home and country: a community which has been continuously present in that land for 2,500 years and for over a thousand years before the advent of Islam; a community which at the turn of the century constituted a third of the population of Baghdad. In fact, Baghdad was sometimes called a Jewish city and some Moslem and Christian shopkeepers would even close on the Jewish feast of Yom Kippur. In a matter of sixty years, Iraq emptied itself of its Iraqi Jews.

Today, we are scattered all over the world and although we left our homes, our schools, our hospitals and our friends behind, we took with us our precious stories, our music, our language and most importantly, our food.

As this book is not the ideal place to write about the history of the Babylonian Jews nor the reasons and the manner in which they had to leave their homeland, I have included, for those who are interested, a few books on that subject, in the selected bibliography.

2. *Afia means health. We say Awafi to someone who is eating a meal and visibly enjoying it. We also use it when someone has just taken a bath.*

The taste of memory

All of us have experienced a 'déjà vu', or should I say a 'déjà tasted' experience at some time in our lives. How often have we eaten something which was pleasantly familiar, transporting us instantaneously to another place far away and long forgotten?

I find myself experiencing just that when I eat ice cream which has been made with rosewater and a type of resin called Saaleb. When the opportunity of eating it comes my way, the experience of 'déjà tasted' renews itself, time and time again, taking me back to our house in Baghdad and to my time in Beirut. Similarly, the distinctive flavour of mastic mixed with chewing gum (available in most Middle Eastern and Greek shops) brings up a picture of my grandmother, her small hands cutting off a piece of mastic to give to me, along with some chewing gum. The smell of jasmine and orange blossom produces the same effect – and I would venture that it transports all of us Middle-Easterners, living in the West, to the fragrant gardens of our childhoods.

Because our senses record minutely what we see, what we touch, hear, smell, taste and feel, and because, as babies, we become acquainted with the outside world through our senses, our taste buds become initiated very fast. These first sensory imprints stay with us all our lives.

As with babies, so I think, with a people or a nation; the food eaten over centuries becomes part of the DNA so to speak, part of a language which lies at the heart of that particular community. Not only does the food we eat define us, it also tells us about our climate, our soil, what grows in our land and what does not grow. In short, it recounts our history as well as our influences and our interaction with the world around us.

Food is more than just nourishment and recipes. It is also a language and an identity.

*Tell me what you eat
and I will tell you what you are.*

Jean Anthelme Brillat-Savarin

*Let nothing which can
be treated by diet
be treated by other means.*

Maimonides

Spices

As much as possible, all spices should be bought whole and only ground when needed.

Baharat

We call all spices *bharat* in Arabic. The Hindi name for India is Bharat and I speculate that a transfer of the name could have occurred, as India was the source of most of the spices that came to Iraq. Very similar to allspice, good supermarkets sell a product called baharat in their herbs and spices section. Packaged in tiny tins, it is a mixture of ground cinnamon, cardamom, nutmeg, paprika, ginger and pepper. It works well with rice dishes, minced meat, chicken and lamb.

Cardamom

We use this warm and pleasant tasting spice in all sorts of dishes, ranging from the savoury to the sweet as well as in some drinks such as tea and coffee. An ancient spice, cardamom originated in southern India, where it is used extensively today in cooking and in Ayurvedic medicine. It is very aromatic and has an unique taste, but once the pods are ground the spice loses its flavour fast. It is therefore better to grind as needed. Cardamom is the third most expensive spice in the world after vanilla and saffron.

Cayenne pepper

This is always in stock in my kitchen. I sprinkle it on some soups and sauces, on grilled or steamed fish and on pasta and some salads. I find cayenne pepper lifts a dish and makes it more interesting.

Cinnamon

Another warming aromatic spice that we use extensively in our dishes. Rich in manganese and calcium, cinnamon was also used for its anti-clotting and anti-fungal action. The early Egyptians used it along with cumin as an embalming agent.

Cumin

An integral part of some Indian, Middle Eastern and North African dishes, cumin is a good source of iron and manganese. It is also used in Ayurvedic medicine to promote digestion and to stimulate the pancreatic enzymes. I drink it as a herbal tea for breakfast. (see p.191).

Sumac

This dark red powder, made from the nut of sour berries, is used in Middle Eastern cooking to give a dish a sour note. I sprinkle it on rice or add it to stews and salads. In Baghdad, we used to buy sumac mixed with za'atar (see below) from street vendors, in small, tightly rolled paper cones. We tipped the sour mixture into our mouths in one or two shots.

Za'atar

This wonderful mixture of toasted sesame seeds, dried thyme, oregano, salt and marjoram has been going for centuries. As early as the twelfth century, Maimonides, the great Jewish philosopher and physician, prescribed za'atar to strengthen the body's immunity. Today, it is readily available in most Middle Eastern shops. You can mix za'atar with olive oil to make a delicious dip, sprinkle it over yoghurts or spice up your kebabs and salads with it.

Sun dried limes *Noomi Basra*

Their name in Arabic translates literally as 'limes from Basra' because they used to arrive at the port of Basra by boat from Iran to be distributed all over Iraq. These dried limes are an important ingredient in our cuisine. We use them in many of our fish and meat dishes for their distinctive sour taste – which differs greatly from ordinary limes or pickled ones. You can buy these wonderfully fragrant limes from any Iranian or Middle Eastern shop. They should be purchased whole and ground as needed, otherwise the flavour evaporates. They make a delicious tea too and are a good remedy for a runny tummy (see p.191).

Salt

Unlike sugar which can be replaced, for example, by grape juice, date syrup or honey, salt is irreplaceable. There is not a fruit, vegetable or mineral that can take the place of salt. It is unique. A humble and pure substance, it has always been one of the most sought after commodities since the inception of civilisation. Homer called it a divine substance. In antiquity it played a vital part in various religious rituals and there are many references to it in the Bible. Considered a purifier and a preserver, both spiritually and physically, salt is used in so many different areas of life, from curing meat and pickling vegetables to softening water and warding off the evil eye!

Although it is no longer expensive to buy, it was once an extremely valuable and precious substance and, until recently, one of the most taxed commodities. The first salt tax, in fact, dates back to 2200 BCE in China. Salt served as money too; coins were made of it in Tibet and China. A bartering commodity, it was more prized than gold. Slaves were traded for salt, hence the expression 'not worth his salt'. People went to war because of it and Roman soldiers were paid in salt. The word for salary comes from salarium, the Latin word for wages which in turn finds its root in sal, Latin for salt. Too much salt kills and a little of it preserves and purifies. The Dead Sea is an example of too much salt; nothing can live in it!

There are many types of salt available on the market. I don't recommend table salt as it usually contains additives such as anti-caking agents and iodine. On the other hand, sea salt, rock salt, Malden salt, kosher salt, 'gris' salt and fleurs de sel, are pure and sold without any additives. Recently, I discovered the wonderful Himalayan salt. Light pink in colour, this salt is mined from the deposits of sediments in the Himalayan mountains.

I use very little salt. That is why I write 'salt to taste' in most of the recipes. How salty you like a dish is a matter of personal choice.

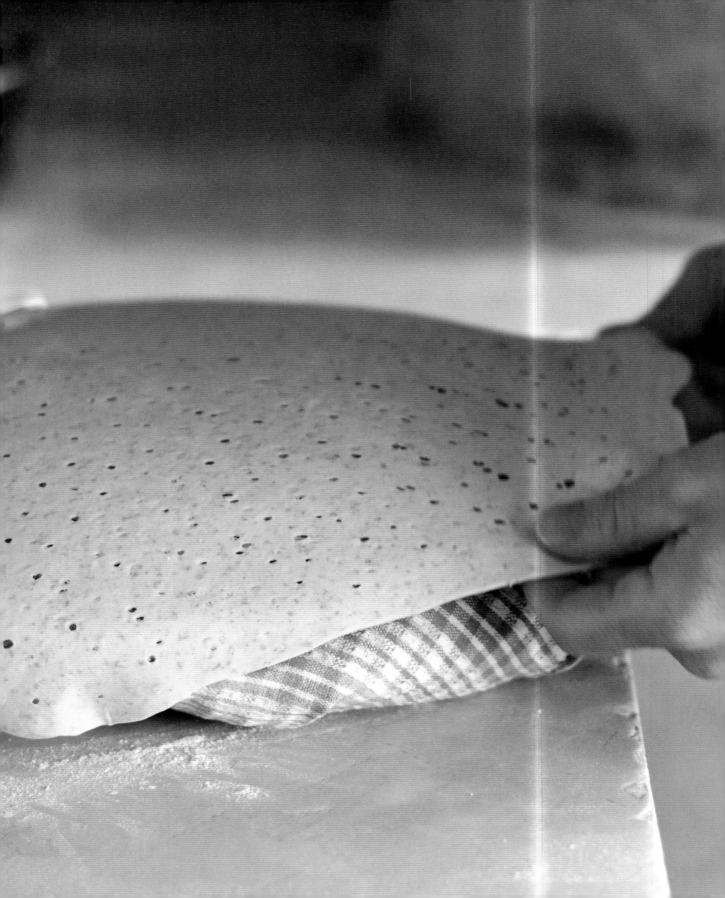

Bread

Khoubez

Bread dates back to the Neolithic period and has come to symbolise all foods, both physically and spiritually.

For us it had a quasi-sacred quality about it. We never threw bread away. We were taught from an early age that, if we should see a piece of bread lying on the ground, we were to pick it up, kiss it and place it on a higher level. It was our way of showing respect for this humble foodstuff. All of us, from the earliest age, had that training; a habit which we progressively lost, once we left Baghdad.

Khoubez is the Arabic name for bread and, in Iraq, we had a few varieties. My favourite was the large, round, flat bread made of whole-wheat flour, which bubbled up on the surface when baked in the clay oven, called *tinnour*. It was delicious eaten hot just on its own or as a wrap with eggs or kebabs and pickles. Another type was an elliptical loaf called *Sammoun*, with pointed ends and a toasted crust, made with white flour. Then, there was a very thin crisp bread called *khoubez Riqaq*, and an unleavened bread which we used to bake for Passover called *khoubez iffteer*; in fact we call the Passover feast in Arabic, *Eid Iffteer* which literally means, the Feast of Unleavened Bread.

Bread accompanied all our meals as did rice.

I used to love watching the making of *Khoubez*. A baker woman would come to our house to bake all things made with dough. She would make *sambousaks* with cheese, date cookies, baklava, *malfoofs* and *ka'akats*. She would roll out the dough thinly and expertly to the required size and shape, stretch it on to a special cushion with which she would slap the dough on the inner wall of the hot *tinnour*. The *khoubez* would be cooked in a matter of minutes, as soon as bubbles were formed on its surface. She would make about 30 pieces, piling each one on top of another, making an impressive sand-coloured column. The delicious aroma of the freshly baked bread always made the whole household hungry.

Starters

Soups salads light dishes and dips

We never had starters as such, in Baghdad. All the dishes were served at the same time, making a sort of buffet on the dining table. Soups were not considered a starter in Iraq but rather as a light meal served with some rice and bread. In winter we sometimes had a bean soup for breakfast. *Shorba*, a mushy rice soup cooked in chicken broth, was made mostly for those who were feeling poorly.

In Beirut, we discovered the convivial and tasty starters called *mezze*. Very much like the Spanish *tapas*, *mezze* (or 'mezza' as the Iraqis pronounce it) is a collection of raw and cooked snacks served in small dishes, usually eaten before the main meal although, sometimes, the *mezze* itself was the main meal! Almost all savoury foods can be part of a *mezze*. In fact, *mezze* food is like picnic food, only served on tables. Introducing different textures and exciting flavours to our palette, it is nibbling *par excellence* and I love that way of eating.

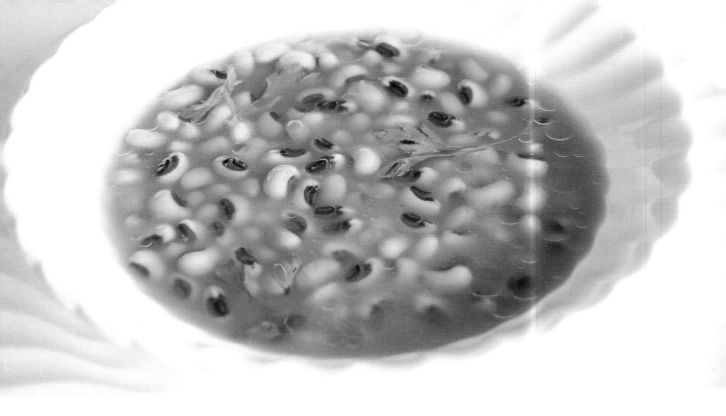

Black-eyed bean soup

Loubia humrah

We used to have this light soup for breakfast during the winters in Baghdad. I still make it, for breakfast, in London. It makes a nice change from porridge!

Serves 4

250g black-eyed beans washed and soaked in
    water overnight
Juice of 1 Seville orange (if not in season use the
    juice of ½ a lemon and ½ an orange)
1 teaspoon chopped mint or flat parsley
1 tablespoon olive oil (optional)
Salt and pepper to taste

Drain the beans and put them in a saucepan. Add water about 2 fingers above the level of the beans and bring to the boil. Boil gently for a few minutes. Skim off any scum from the surface. Reduce the heat, cover and simmer gently for 25 minutes or until cooked.

There should be some reddish liquid left, just covering the beans (if not top up with a little more water). Add the flat parsley or mint, the orange juice, lemon juice and olive oil. Mix well, season and serve hot as a soup for breakfast or dinner.

Variation: add one finely chopped spring onion to cook with the beans and **either** half a chopped tomato **or** a few chopped lemon and orange segments as garnish.

Lentil soup
Shorbat addas

I add a carrots to this recipe because the sweetness of the carrots enhances the flavour of the lentils. The addition of preserved lemons gives this humble soup an interesting twist.

Serves 4

300ml red lentils washed and soaked
About 1 litre of water
1 large onion, finely chopped
2 small grated carrots
1 teaspoon stock powder or Swiss
   Bouillon powder
1 garlic clove, peeled
A pinch of cayenne pepper
½ teaspoon salt or to taste
A pinch or more ground cumin
½ preserved lemon cut in small pieces (p.162)
1 tablespoon lemon or lime juice.
2 tablespoons olive oil
Coriander leaves for the garnish

Wash the lentils and drain.

Heat a little oil in a saucepan and sauté the onion until lightly golden. Add the preserved lemon and stir. Add the lentils, then the grated carrot and stir-fry for 5 minutes.

In a jug mix the vegetable stock cube or powder, with the water to make the stock. Add the stock, salt, garlic clove, cayenne pepper and cumin to the lentils and mix well. Cover and cook on moderate heat for 25 minutes or until cooked. Then use a blender to purée the mixture. Add some water if you find the consistency too thick. Simmer for another ten minutes or so.

Before serving, mix in the lemon or lime juice and olive oil.

Garnish with some coriander leaves.

Sesame butter
Tahina

From the Arabic word to grind, *tahina* or *tahini* is a thick oily paste made from ground sesame seeds. A basic ingredient of Middle Eastern cuisine, it has a nutty flavour similar to peanut butter and can be used as a spread or mixed in salad dressings, with fish or meat and in dips such as *houmus*.

In Iraq we used to sweeten it with date syrup smeared on a piece of bread. My husband, Frank, continues to do just that every morning for breakfast and, for a change, I sometimes mix it with cinnamon and honey which I find go very well together. I like to keep the *tahina* paste in the refrigerator even though, unlike many other oils, its oil is known for its wonderful resistance to rancidity.

Sesame seeds are very nutritious; they provide us with a high quality unsaturated oil and a good dose of calcium, zinc, magnesium and vitamin B.

DATE SYRUP

TAH
EXT

Net weight / P

Tahina and cinnamon spread

This is a delicious and nutritious mixture, easy and quick to make for breakfast. Children love it, as it looks like milk chocolate and has a sweet and nutty taste. It is a good alternative to jam and other sweet spreads containing sugar.

> **2 tablespoons agave or honey**
> **4 to 5 tablespoons ground cinnamon**
> **1 or 2 tablespoons water**
> **4 to 5 tablespoons sesame paste (*tahina*)**

Mix the agave (or honey) together with the cinnamon until you get a smooth dark paste. Add the *Tahina* and mix thoroughly. Taste and adjust the flavour.

Spread generously over toast or a chunk of fresh bread.

Tahina and banana spread

A creamy, child-friendly paste to be spread on toast, bread and rice cakes. A mixture of banana, *tahina* and yoghurt, it is packed with essential nutrients and great for breakfast.

> **1 ripe banana**
> **5 to 6 tablespoons sesame paste (*tahina*)**
> **4 to 5 tablespoons or more of yoghurt (or soya milk)**

Mash the banana then add five to six tablespoons of *tahina* and mix thoroughly. You will end up with a thick paste, similar to peanut butter in consistency. (You can add more *tahina* if you wish).

Add the yoghurt and mix again. This will soften the texture (if you find the spread too thick add a tablespoon of milk or water).

Humous with *tahina*

Humous b'thina

Make your own chickpea dip and enjoy it as a snack with bread or some sliced carrots and celery sticks.

> **250g dried chickpeas**
> **6 or more tablespoons sesame paste (*tahina*)**
> **2 to 3 tablespoons lemon juice**
> **1 or 2 garlic cloves**
> **2 tablespoons olive oil**
> **½ teaspoon salt or to taste**
> **A sprinkling of paprika**

Wash and soak the chickpeas overnight in a saucepan.

The next day place the saucepan with the chickpeas and water on a medium heat and cook or about 1 hour or more. You want them to be soft.

In a bowl, mash the chickpeas with a fork or a blender to a granular or smooth paste.

Crush the garlic with some salt and add to the chickpea paste with the lemon juice and the *tahina.* Mix in the olive oil and stir into a creamy consistency. If you find the paste too thick just add a little more olive oil or some water.

Adjust the taste before serving, sprinkle with paprika and garnish with some chopped flat parsley.

Olive oil dip with *za'atar*

Za'atar wa zeyt

If you are feeling a bit peckish and want a quick savoury snack, put away those crisps. I've got just the thing for you. Mix some *za'atar* and olive oil on a plate and mop it up with a warm piece of bread. I guarantee it will satisfy your craving. I have it sometimes for breakfast or as a delicious pick-me-up, whenever I feel like tasting something different.

1 to 2 spoonfuls of *za'atar*
Lots of extra virgin olive oil

Pour some olive oil on a plate and sprinkle the *za'atar* over it. Serve it with some hot pitta bread.

Strained yoghurt

Laban manashaf

Laban manashaf literally translates from the Arabic as 'dried yoghurt'. It is very much like thick cream or soft cheese in consistency, depending on how much of its liquid filters out. This is how we used to make it in Baghdad. My grandmother would pour a quantity of yoghurt into a white muslin bag and hang it on the kitchen tap for its liquid to flow out. I remember seeing the puffed up bag shrivel slowly as the whey dripped rhythmically into the sink.

Serves 2 to 4

900g goat's yoghurt or any other that you prefer
A muslin or cheese cloth
4 to 6 tablespoons of olive oil
1 or 2 tablespoons *za'atar* (p.25) (optional)
½ teaspoon salt or to taste

Mix the salt with the yoghurt.

Spread the muslin in a bowl and pour the yoghurt into it. Gather the muslin cloth around the yoghurt and make a knot at the top or close tightly with a rubber band. Hang over the sink by making another knot and attaching it on to the tap. Leave it for about 4 to 5 hours or overnight. (The longer you leave it the drier the texture.)

Once the liquid or whey has filtered out, place the cream cheese on a plate, make a large hole in the centre and pour in the olive oil. Sprinkle with *za'ater* if desired. You can also sweeten it with jam or honey and spread it on a piece of bread. Serve it for breakfast or eat as a snack.

Variation: For a quicker way which does not entail the washing of the muslin cloth afterwards, use a disposable coffee filter or three layers of paper towel. Line a funnel with the filter or paper towels and place over an empty jar. Pour in the yoghurt and leave overnight in the refrigerator. If you like your cream cheese slightly sour leave it out in the kitchen.

Stormy cheese omelette
Ajjat b' jebben

Ajjat b' jebben literally translates as 'a cheese storm'. Delicious to eat hot or cold accompanied by a salad or sweetened with a dollop of jam.

Serves 2 to 3

4 free range eggs
180g grated *haloumi* or cheddar cheese
2 tablespoons of milk or water
1 tablespoon olive oil
Pepper to taste

Beat the eggs in a bowl. Add the grated cheese and the milk and mix well.

With a paper towel wipe a non-stick frying pan with some olive oil. Heat the pan and pour in the egg mixture. Stir with a wooden spoon and allow some of the runny egg to set. Then reduce the heat to low and cover. Cook for 10 minutes.

Uncover and check with a spatula if the bottom has turned golden brown (if not, cook for a few more minutes) and then transfer to a preheated grill. Cook until the top turns golden brown.

Serve hot or cold, cut in triangles like a cake. I like it with bread and apricot or Pomelo preserve.

Variation: Instead of putting the pan under the grill turn the omelette to brown the other side. If the omelette is too large and awkward to turn, do the following: place a flat plate firmly on top of the pan and turn the whole thing upside down. (The browned side should be on top.) Now slide the omelette back in the pan so that the reverse side cooks for another 5 to 10 minutes on low heat.

Scrambled eggs with spinach
M'farka

This is one of the many Babylonian specialities that I love to eat for breakfast or as a light lunch, because it is so easy to rustle up. The steamed spinach with the egg makes a delicious combination. I use baby spinach because of its delicate flavour; mature spinach is stronger and also requires more work removing the middle stalks.

Serves 2

2 eggs lightly beaten
100g baby spinach washed and drained
1 medium onion finely chopped
1 tablespoon of olive oil
Salt and pepper to taste

Sauté the onion until soft and golden. Throw in the spinach and stir-fry until it becomes very limp and the water has evaporated. Add a little salt and pepper. Pour in the beaten eggs and keep stirring to mix. Cook for about five minutes or until the eggs are cooked but still soft and fluffy.

Serve hot or cold with some warm pitta bread.

Variation 1: This is great with the addition of some mushrooms. Stir fry with the sautéed onions for a few minutes. Then add the spinach and continue as above.

Variation 2: This version is with tomatoes, we call it *Beyth b'tamata.* Sauté the onions as above. Throw in 2 finely chopped tomatoes and stir-fry until soft. Season with salt and cayenne pepper. Pour in the 2 beaten eggs. Keep stirring to mix and scramble. Cook for 3 to 4 minutes or until the eggs are cooked, but still soft and fluffy.

Potato egg fritters

Beith (bala) laham

With this recipe you can make small fritters or, to save time, one thick and large omelette which can be cut into portions like a cake.

Serves 4 to 6

6 eggs lightly beaten
3 to 4 potatoes, cut into very small cubes
1 bunch spring onions, finely chopped
1 small red pepper, finely diced
1 small green pepper, finely diced
Half a large bunch of flat parsley, finely chopped
1 teaspoon ground cumin
1 teaspoon curry powder
Salt and pepper, to taste

Steam the potatoes until cooked. Set aside to cool.

In a large bowl, put the cooled potatoes, spring onions, red and green peppers and the flat parsley. Add the cumin, curry powder, salt and pepper, and mix well. Then pour in the beaten eggs and mix. The mixture should be soft but not watery. (If needs be add another egg).

In a frying pan, heat a little oil on medium heat. Drop a spoonful (the size of a serving spoon) of the mixture into the hot oil and, with the back of a spoon, lightly flatten the mixture, cooking each side until golden brown. Cook in batches, a few at a time, transferring on to kitchen paper to absorb the excess oil.

Serve with a tomato or cucumber salad and some pickles.

Variation 1: Heat a little oil in a frying pan (23cm). Pour in the egg mixture and cook covered on medium low heat until the bottom has turned golden brown. Then, place under the grill to cook the top.

Variation 2: You can also use any leftover vegetables in this recipe.

Green egg tortilla

Beyth b'mkhadar

We make this green omelette a lot. It is a family favourite for a light meal accompanied by a salad and some mango pickle.

Serves 2

4 medium eggs. lightly beaten
100g frozen peas
1 small courgette cut into very small cubes
A large handful of flat parsley, finely chopped
4 spring onions, finely chopped
1 tablespoon oilive oil for the mixture
Some oil for frying
½ teaspoon vegetable cube or Bouillon powder
¼ teaspoon cayenne pepper
¼ teaspoon cumin
½ teaspoon salt or to taste

Heat a little oil in a frying pan and add the courgettes and peas. Cover and cook for about 5 minutes on medium heat, stirring occasionally. Set aside to cool.

Combine all the ingredients with the eggs and mix. Heat a little oil in a non-stick frying pan (18cm wide) and pour in the egg mixture. Cook, covered, on a medium-low heat until the bottom has turned golden brown. Then place under the grill to cook the top.

Variation: you can add some finely sliced mushrooms to this. Stir-fry the mushrooms with the peas and courgettes until soft. Add to the mixture, once cooled.

Slow cooked brown eggs
Beyth al t'beet

Every Saturday morning in Baghdad, we had these wonderful eggs for breakfast, accompanied by thin slivers of raw onion and a spicy tomato and mango pickle salad.

Cooked overnight, for at least twelve hours, these brown eggs were the traditional breakfast staple of all the Babylonian Jews of Iraq. On Friday afternoons, when preparing to cook the Sabbath meal which consisted of chicken and rice, my grandmother would place a dozen eggs on the lid of a large cauldron to cook in the steam of the chicken that was inside. The eggs would be covered with another lid and the whole construction wrapped in numerous towels to keep the heat from escaping (very much like a tea cosy) and left to cook slowly on charcoal embers until the next morning.

Cooking thus, the egg whites turned brown and their taste transformed into a delicious, deep flavour which you only get with slow cooking.

Pre-heated the oven to 150°C/Gas Mark 2.

Meanwhile, boil the eggs for 10 minutes.

Put them in a steamer with a little water in the bottom pot and cover. Place in the oven and bake for 3 to 4 hours.

Variation: Put the raw eggs in a steamer with some water in the bottom pot and bring to the boil. Let the water boil gently for 30 minutes, then reduce the heat to very low. Leave them to steam for at least 5 hours or so. You can leave the eggs for the whole day too but make sure there is enough water in the pot, at all times.

Whichever way you decide to cook them, the eggs will keep for at least 3 days in the refrigerator.

Slow baked egg sandwich

Laffa beyth al t'beet

This is no ordinary egg sandwich. Consisting of flat parsley, mango pickle, tomato and a slow baked brown egg, this delicious pitta bread sandwich will excite your taste buds and satisfy your hunger in minutes.

Half a wholemeal pitta bread warmed in a toaster
1 *t'beet* egg (see p.51)
A spoon or two of the spicy tomato and mango salad (p.69)
Salt to taste

Cut the egg in half and stuff it in the warm pitta. Spoon in some salad and munch with relish.

Variation 1: If you are in a hurry and cannot be bothered to make the salad, just add a slice of tomato, a slice of pickled mango from the bottle with some flat parsley.

Variation 2: Instead of the mango you can use *Turshi* pickle (p.161).

Dried broad beans stew

Ful M'dammas

This vegetarian dish of small broad beans is usually served for breakfast with tomatoes, flat parsley and a chopped boiled egg. It can also be an appetiser amongst an array of other small dishes. I usually make it as part of my weekend brunch menu. You can buy the dried broad beans from all Middle Eastern or Indian shops. They come in two sizes, large beans and baby ones. I have a preference for the small ones.

Serves 4

250g small dried broad beans soaked overnight
A handful of chopped flat parsley
2 garlic cloves, peeled
Juice of 1 lemon
3 or 4 tablespoons olive oil
Salt and pepper to taste

Wash the beans and soak overnight.

The next day, drain the beans and tip them in a saucepan with the garlic cloves and cover with water, about 5cm above the beans. Bring to the boil. Once the water starts boiling, turn the heat down to a simmer, half cover and cook for about 1 hour or until the beans are soft. During that time, check the water level. The beans should always have a little water covering them.

When cooking time is over, the excess water should have evaporated leaving a creamy liquid sludge and very soft beans (add water if too dry).

About 10 minutes before serving add the chopped flat parsley, lemon juice, olive oil, salt and pepper and mix well. (Do not be tempted to add the lemon juice whilst the beans are cooking as this will harden them.)

Serve warm with some pitta bread. You can accompany the beans with some finely chopped tomatoes, hard-boiled eggs and slices of onion. This makes a delicious light meal or snack.

Haloumi and shallot sandwich
Jeben Wa Basal

Imagine a warm pitta stuffed with hot slivers of *haloumi* cheese and soft, cooked shallots. Pick one up and bite gently into its warm layers. Awesome. Pure bliss!

Don't be fooled, this is not a mere sandwich; that would be an insult to this hearty snack. In fact, it is considered by many to be a very satisfying meal. We used to have this for breakfast in Baghdad. The cheese we used was made from sheep's milk and stored in jars full of brine. As a result, it was quite salty, so simmering it in boiling water stripped it of the excess salt and softened it. The cheese and shallots were served in the water they were cooked in, accompanied by a bowl of date syrup or a plate of sliced cucumbers and flat parsley.

Serves 4

200g *haloumi* cheese, sliced
Half a cucumber, thinly sliced
5 small shallots or onions, sliced in half
Brown pitta bread
Flat parsley

Peel the shallots, halve them and place in boiling water and bring to the boil. Turn down to a simmer. Cook for 10 to 15 minutes or until soft but still firm. Add the sliced cheese and simmer for a further 10 minutes.

Meanwhile, warm the pitta bread and slice in half.

Serve the cheese and shallots in a bowl with its hot water. Fill the pitta. Garnish with the sliced cucumber and flat parsley.

Lettuce

Khas

The Greeks and Romans considered lettuce to be mildly soporific due to a milky fluid in its stem called Lactucarium. So they had lettuce at the end of a meal to prepare them for a good night's sleep. That said, there are those who believe it opens up one's appetite and so they have a lettuce salad at the beginning of a meal.

We never used lettuce leaves in our salads in Baghdad. We had the whole lettuce served on a plate along with whole tomatoes, cucumbers, spring onions, bunches of flat parsley and other herbs. These would be eaten as one would crudités. Lettuce was also eaten at any time of the day to quench one's thirst or as a refreshing snack. Street vendors would wash a whole load in the Tigris River and then sell them to passers by.

Khas is the general name for lettuce in Arabic. There are those who say that the English name Cos comes from the Arabic Khas, describing the long-leafed variety that grows in the Middle East; others believe the name comes from the Greek island of Kos where the same type of lettuce grows. Either or both propositions could be correct and this does indicate one thing at least, that the Cos variety came to Europe from the East.

Tomato and lemon salad

Tamata wa noumi hameth

Tip: Before squeezing a lemon, press firmly and roll it on your work top. This will make it easier to get more juice out of it, quickly.

We did not have sour lemons in Baghdad. We had limes and sweet lemons which we called *noumi helou*. Sweet lemons were larger than ordinary lemons and rounder, not unlike oranges. They were not sour at all and had a delicate sweet flavour.

We had oranges and sour oranges which we called *narenj*. These were quite sour and a little bitter, very similar to Seville oranges. In fact, the Spanish for orange is *naranja* which comes from the Arabic word *narenj*. We used *narenj* in salads and for cooking.

Serves 2

2 ripe juicy tomatoes
1 lemon
A sprinkling of salt

Chop the tomatoes into small pieces (about 1cm).

Wash the lemon and peel the skin and pith. Cut out the segments and slice each one into three pieces. Make sure you take out the pips. Sprinkle with a little salt. Mix well. Refrigerate for 10 minutes before serving.

Tomato and cucumber salad
Tamata wa khyar

Serves 2

1 ripe beefsteak tomato
2 small Mediterranean cucumbers or half a large one
2 tablespoons coarsely chopped flat parsley
1 teaspoon lemon juice
1 teaspoon orange juice
2 tablespoons olive oil
Salt to taste

Slice the tomatoes, place in a bowl and sprinkle with a little salt. Let them rest for 10 to 15 minutes so that their juices start oozing out.

Meanwhile, peel and cut the cucumbers into small chunks.

Mix the tomatoes, cucumbers, the lemon and orange juice, olive oil and flat parsley. Adjust the seasoning to your taste and serve.

Beetroot salad

Zalatat shwander

Serves 4

4 medium sized beetroots
Juice of 1 lemon
3 tablespoons olive oil
Salt and pepper to taste
Flat parsley, finely chopped
**   for the garnish**

I usually bake the beetroots for this salad but you can also steam them. However, I do not recommend boiling because you lose a lot of the nutrients that way.

Pre-heat the oven to 190°C/Gas Mark 5.

Wash the beetroots thoroughly. Wrap each one in aluminium foil. Place them on a baking tray and bake for about an hour or so.

When cooked, unwrap and allow to cool.

Then peel and slice the beetroots. (Do not slice them before they are cooked as their juice will seep out.) Arrange them in a dish, add the lemon juice and parsley and season with salt and pepper. Drizzle with olive oil.

Variation: Cut the beetroots into cubes, using the same dressing as above, mix in a tablespoon or two of chopped fresh ginger.

Cucumber salad
Zlatat el khyar

In Baghdad we used to finely slice the cucumbers, salt them and set them aside for about 30 minutes. Once limp, the excess juice was squeezed out; they were then dressed with vinegar and sugar. In my version, I use a mandolin to slice the cucumbers paper thin, so no need to squeeze out their juice to make them limp. Also, this way they retain all their goodness.

Serves 4

400g small cucumbers (small Middle Eastern ones, preferably)
3 tablespoons lime juice
3 tablespoons cider or white vinegar
¾ teaspoon salt or to taste
3 teaspoons sugar (or agave)
1 tablespoon water

Wash the cucumbers and, using a mandolin or a sharp knife, cut them into wafer-thin slices.

Mix all the dressing ingredients in a salad bowl with the cucumbers. Taste to adjust the flavour.

Serve immediately or set aside in the refrigerator. If you set aside, the cucumbers will start to release their juices after a while, making the dressing more watery. I quite like that, but if you don't, **either** serve immediately **or** salt the cucumber slices before use and set aside for 20 minutes for the juices to drain out. Then squeeze the slices, a handful at a time, and place in a salad bowl.

Variation: I like to add a big pinch of cayenne pepper or half a small chilli, finely chopped and 2 sliced shallots to the cucumbers. Their individual flavours sing well together.

Cabbage salad

Zlatat lahana

For this salad you want the cabbage to be soft. In Baghdad, the cabbage would be finely sliced, sprinkled with a lot of salt and put under the hot sun to speed up the softening process. Once limp, the excess liquid was squeezed out and the cabbage dressed with lemon juice and sugar. This winter salad accompanied *t'beet* eggs (p.51) or kebabs.

Today, a quicker way would be to shred the cabbage in a food processor. This softens it, making it possible to squeeze out the excess water right away. All you need to do then is to dress it with lemon juice and sugar.

Serves 6

1 spring cabbage
Juice of 1 lemons
Juice of 1 orange
2 tablespoons sugar or agave

Serve garnished with rocket leaves, flat parsley, spring onions and small cubed tomatoes for colour.

Variation: A nice change would be to use peppercorns and cider vinegar in the dressing. This is an easy and quick recipe packed with subtle flavours.

> 1 **spring cabbage**
> ½ **teaspoon green peppercorns in brine**
> 1½ **tablespoon cider vinegar**
> 4 **tablespoons olive oil**
> 1 **tablespoon lemon juice**
> **Salt and pepper to taste**

Shred the cabbage finely. I prefer to do this with a mandolin as it produces consistently fine slices, but you can use a sharp knife.

Steam the cabbage for about five to six minutes or until it has wilted slightly. Do not steam it too long as the bright emerald green colour will fade.

Arrange on a serving dish and let it cool down a little. Mix the dressing ingredients with the peppercorns, pour over the cabbage and toss gently. Taste and adjust the flavour.

Serve warm or at room temperature.

Mango pickle and tomato salad
Amba wa tamata

In summer, when the tomatoes were in season this salad was always served with the slow cooked *t'beet* eggs (p.51). In winter, we served the eggs with a cabbage salad instead.

Serves 2 to 4

2 ripe tomatoes cut into small cubes
2 slices of pickled mango finely chopped
A handful of flat parsley, finely chopped
Salt to taste

Place all the ingredients in a bowl and mix.

Chickpeas

Houmus

These peas are a street food we call *lablabi*. The street vendors in Baghdad used to shout '*lablabi*, hot boiled chickpeas', at every street corner. Ali, the chickpea seller, used to park his trolley outside our school every afternoon and wait for the hungry pupils to spill out. When our lessons were over, he was literally mobbed by all those wanting to eat a bowlful of his peas. I still have a picture in my mind's eye of Ali dishing out piping hot chickpeas into tiny bowls, sprinkling them with salt before handing them over to us. We would eat these on the hop before going home.

A high fibre legume, chickpeas – Bengal grams or *garbanzos* as they are sometimes called – originated in the Middle East and were first cultivated there about 5000 years ago, before spreading to the Indian sub-continent and parts of Africa.

The light brown ones are the most common but there are other varieties which are black, red, brown and green. Chickpeas are sold either dried or canned. If you are using the dried ones, pre-soaking is mandatory. If you are in a rush or have forgotten to soak the peas beforehand, you can resort to the canned ones.

My chickpea salad

Serves 4

250g dried chickpeas, soaked
  overnight
1 fresh tomato finely chopped
A handful of finely chopped
  fresh coriander

The Dressing

Half a preserved lemon, finely
  chopped (seep.162)
4 tablespoons lemon juice
6 tablespoons of extra virgin
  olive oil
½ teaspoon salt or to taste
¼ teaspoon cayenne pepper

We used to eat the boiled chickpeas with just a dash of salt. In this recipe, I have added a spicy dressing with cayenne pepper, combined with some preserved lemon and fresh coriander, making an intensely flavoured salad out of this humble legume.

Drain the soaked chickpeas and place in a saucepan. Cover with water and bring to the boil. Turn down to a medium heat, half cover and cook for about 1 hour 15 minutes. The peas should be soft but not mushy. Drain and leave aside to cool down.

Meanwhile, mix the dressing ingredients in a salad bowl. Combine the cooled chickpeas with the dressing and mix well. At this point taste and adjust the seasoning and tartness.

Add the tomatoes and chopped coriander and give the whole salad a good mix.

Variation 1: If you do not have preserved lemons you can add the zest of 1 lemon instead. Use some chopped fresh flat parsley if you prefer it to coriander.

Variation 2: This has yoghurt added to the dressing. Boil the chickpeas as above and set aside to cool. In a bowl, add a crushed garlic clove, half teaspoon salt, 3 tablespoons lemon juice, 5 tablespoons olive oil and 200g thick goat's or Greek yoghurt. Give the lot a good stir. Tip in the cooled chickpeas and mix. Add 1 small chopped tomato, sprinkle with a quarter teaspoon cayenne pepper and a handful of chopped flat parsley. The taste is truly amazing. Try it!

Tabbouleh

Tabboula

Burghul is made of kernels of wheat (whole or hulled) which have been boiled, dried and crushed into three different grades: coarse, medium and fine. It was prepared in this way more than 5000 years ago by the ancient people of the Middle East. Fine *burghul* is used to make this *tabbouleh* salad.

Very popular in Iraq, *tabbouleh* originated in Lebanon and was adopted very quickly all over the Middle East. Our Lebanese cook, Marie, taught us this recipe whilst we were living in Beirut. It contains more *burghul* than the usual *tabbouleh* served in restaurants.

Serves 4

150g fine *burghul*
14 tablespoons finely chopped flat parsley
7 tablespoons mint leaves, finely chopped
2 fresh tomatoes, finely diced
2 spring onions, finely chopped
9 tablespoons lemon juice
9 tablespoons extra virgin olive oil
½ teaspoon salt or to taste
Ground pepper

Wash the *burghul* and soak for about 5 to 10 minutes. Then drain and squeeze out the excess water. Tip into a salad bowl and fluff up with a fork.

Chop the flat parsley, mint and spring onions and mix with the *burghul*. Add the tomatoes, the lemon juice, salt, pepper and olive oil and mix well. Taste and adjust the seasoning.

Serve immediately, otherwise add the tomatoes just before serving.

Mains

Chicken

Chicken

All Iraqis ate more or less the same food. Over the years each religious group developed their way of cooking certain dishes and invented others which were typical of their community. For the Babylonian Jews the most important dish was their emblematic Sabbath meal called *T'beet*. This chicken dish is to the Sabbath what turkey is to Christmas and Thanksgiving with one exception; we had it every Saturday, fifty-two times a year.

As no cooking or any kind of work is permitted on Saturdays, all the preparations for the Sabbath meal were done the day before. An ingenious method of slow cooking was devised whereby a whole chicken, stuffed with rice and spices, buried almost completely in rice, was cooked in a large pot overnight and for over 12 hours. A dozen eggs were placed on the lid of the pot to cook in its heat and steam; these would be covered with another lid which in turn was covered in numerous towels to keep the heat from escaping (very much like a tea cosy) and left to cook slowly on charcoal embers until the next morning. This method provided hot brown *T'beet* eggs for breakfast and a hot meal for lunch. The slow cooking gave the dish a much richer and deeper flavour.

Overnight chicken buried in aromatic rice

T'beet

The name for this Sabbath dish comes from the Arabic *tabayit* which means to stay overnight, which is how long *t'beet* used to be cooked. This is my grandmother's recipe which my mother continues to use when making her delicious *t'beet*. It is the traditional way to make this sumptuous dish. It might seem a lengthy process at first but you'll soon get the hang of it. The chicken is cooked first, then the rice is added and cooked together with the chicken. It is worth the effort and makes a spectacular party dish.

Serves 6 to 8

1.5 to 2 kg chicken
2 to 3 pieces of cut lemon to rub the chicken
White Basmati rice (700ml level in a measuring jug)
3 tablespoons olive oil
1 small onion, finely chopped
1 fresh tomato, finely chopped
2 tablespoons tomato paste
1 cube chicken stock or teaspoon Bouillon powder
4 whole cardamom pods
1 tablespoon salt
Pepper to taste

The Stuffing
2 to 3 tablespoons Basmati rice
3 tablespoons chopped chicken (optional)
1 large fresh tomato, diced
1 tablespoon olive oil
1 tablespoon ground cardamom
1 tablespoon ground cinnamon
Salt and pepper to taste

To get the best flavour I recommend a free range mature boiler chicken which is an older bird than the usual roaster. Its taste is deeper and meatier. A free range roaster will do too.

Wash and soak both quantities of rice in 2 separate bowls for 30 minutes.

Wash the whole chicken (leaving the skin on). Cut off the tip of the parson's nose and pat dry. Rub the chicken inside and out with a piece of cut lemon. This helps to clean it and remove any unpleasant odours.

Combine all the stuffing ingredients and stuff the chicken, then close the opening with a skewer (loosely stuff the inside as the rice expands to double its size).

In a heavy-bottomed pot, heat the oil and sauté the chopped onion until limp and transparent. Stir in the chopped tomato and salt and continue cooking for 2 minutes.

Now pop the chicken in the pot (with no liquid) and cook covered, on medium heat, turning occasionally, until golden all over. (If necessary, add a few drops of water.) This will take about 25 minutes. Liberally prick the chicken so as to allow the juices to flow out.

Pour boiling water over the whole chicken, covering half of it. Stir in the tomato paste, the chicken cube, the cardamom pods and the salt. (You can add a stick of celery that you will discard later.) Cook for about 1 hour (a little more if it is a boiler).

Take the chicken out of the pan. Measure the remaining liquid. You should have 700ml. If less, top it up.

Put the chicken back in the pot. Bring to the boil and add the rice around the chicken. Bring to the boil again. Then reduce the heat to low, cover and cook for 20 to 25 minutes. (It is best not to uncover the pot at this stage.)

Now turn the heat to a minimum and place a heat diffuser beneath the pan and cook for another 20 minutes.

Then either transfer the pot to a preheated oven at 80°C/Gas Mark ¼ and slow cook for another 2 hours or more (remember, this used to cook for 12 hours in Baghdad) or continue to cook on the stove.

Before serving immerse the bottom of the pot in cold water. This will make it easier to detach the *h'kaka* (bottom crust). Spoon the *t'beet* into a large serving dish, with the chicken in the middle and the crust on top.

Variation: I have eaten this dish made with 750g of shredded pieces of lamb and it was delicious too. Sauté the chopped onion, brown the meat, then stir in the **stuffing spices** (except for the rice, of course). Add 750ml water, 2 tablespoons olive oil, 2 tablespoons tomato paste, 1 cube chicken stock or teaspoon Bouillon powder, 4 cardamom pods, 1 tablespoon salt and pepper to taste. Bring to the boil, pour in the rice and stir to mix. Bring back to the boil. Cover and cook on a low heat for 20 minutes and proceed to slow cook as above. Serve hot.

Chicken with potatoes in a light soup

Marag b'jeej

This is another one of my mother's specialities. You serve this dish as a light clear soup or as a main meal with some rice. I recommend a free range mature boiler chicken, which is an older bird than the usual roaster. Its taste is deeper and meatier. A free range roaster will do too.

Wash the whole chicken (leaving the skin on). Cut off the entire parson's nose and pat dry. Rub the chicken inside and out with a piece of cut lemon. This helps to clean it and remove any unpleasant odours. Cut into 8 to 10 pieces. (If too difficult when raw, you can do that once the chicken has cooked a little).

Combine all the ingredients in a large pot (except the potatoes). Turn down to a simmer and cook for 15 minutes *without any water*, browning the chicken pieces on all sides. Be careful not to burn them. Liberally prick the chicken pieces so as to allow their juices to flow out. Simmer for a further 5 minutes or until all the liquid has evaporated.

Meanwhile, boil a sufficient amount of water to cover the chicken pieces. Pour the boiling water over the chicken. Cover and simmer for 50 minutes if a roaster (90 minutes if a boiler chicken) or until the chicken is very tender. Add the potatoes and simmer covered for another 25 minutes or until the potatoes are cooked and the liquid has reduced to a thick broth.

Serve with plain rice. Alternatively, the dish can be served as a clear soup by adding more liquid to the pot and lightly shredding the chicken.

Variation: You can add chickpeas or peas to the broth and serve the dish like a stew, rather than a soup.

Serves 6 to 8

1.5 kg chicken
1 onion, finely chopped
1 fresh tomato, finely chopped
¼ teaspoon cayenne pepper (optional)
2 whole cardamom pods (optional)
2 large potatoes, peeled and cut into medium sized chunks
Salt and pepper to taste

Rice

Rice

'A meal without rice is not a meal, it's a snack'

'The Arabic for rice is *ruz* – but the Iraqis call it *timman*.

We had rice with every meal in Baghdad. It was an indispensable accompaniment to all our dishes. I have memories of our cook sifting and washing the rice to clean it of impurities and starch – a ritual performed every morning in preparation for the midday meal. Later on, while it was cooking, its delicious aroma would waft through our house and make us all very hungry.

The earliest cultivation of rice is believed to have taken place in north east India around 4000 BCE and, much later, in Vietnam, China and other parts of the Far East. Today, rice is grown all over the world. Considered a symbol of fertility in some cultures, rice is showered on newly weds for good luck and a plentiful family life. There are hundreds of varieties: long grain, short grain, sticky, fluffy, fragrant, white, brown, red, black and many others. *Basmati* is now the best known Indian variety in the West; a fragrant, long grained rice, its name in Hindi means 'the queen of fragrance'.

The most prized variety in Iraq was the *Ambar* rice. Slightly golden in colour and very aromatic, it was cultivated for home use only and not for export. *Basmati* rice is a good substitute for our dishes. For *Kubba* shells (p.108) or desserts, use a starchy ground rice or short grain rice because these do not collapse when cooked.

There are many ways to cook rice. You can boil it like pasta with a lot of water or half cook it, drain it and then let it steam in the oven. You can stir-fry it, bake it, grind it and use it in puddings and other desserts. The list is too long. The one thing you should not be is afraid of cooking rice. Just follow these basic guidelines and you will be turning out amazingly fancy rice dishes in no time.

The six guidelines

1. A heavy-bottomed pot

If you cook the rice in a heavy-bottomed pot it will not burn at the bottom. I do not use aluminium. Enamel and cast iron pots are fine or, as I prefer, stainless steel or non-stick.

2. A tight fitting lid

It is essential that the pot has a tight fitting lid. This is because rice cooks also in its steam and if steam is allowed to escape, the rice will cook unevenly. You can easily make almost any lid tight by putting a sheet of aluminium foil between it and the pot. Arrange the foil over the pot and gently lay down the lid. Then scrunch the foil tightly all the way round to make it as airtight as possible.

3. Washing and soaking

Rice must be copiously washed to remove the starch or the rice grains will stick together. The secret is to wash the rice until the water is no longer cloudy. Soaking swells the grains, which reduces the amount of water and cooking time.

It also helps to make the rice fluffier. Some people soak overnight but 30 minutes to one hour is usually sufficient. Discard the water you soak it in.

4. Amount of water

If you have washed and soaked your rice as above, the proportion of water to rice is 1¼ measure of water to 1 measure of rice. If you have washed but not soaked, use 1½ measure of water. Another more *ad hoc* method which works well is to add water to 2 fingers above the level of the rice.

One thing to bear in mind, there are many varieties of rice and, indeed, of *Basmati* rice. Each cooks slightly differently, varying by just a few minutes in some cases. In addition your pots and ovens might differ from mine, so you must experiment within these guidelines to see what works for you in your own environment.

5. Minimum heat

When the recipe calls for cooking on minimum heat it is so that the rice can cook slowly and thoroughly without burning. Gas hobs are not as sensitive as say, electric or induction. A good work-around is to employ a heat diffuser beneath the pot.

6. Never uncover prematurely

Well that depends on the recipe but it is a golden rule nonetheless. It is not rocket science – if you let out the steam before the time is up – the rice will cook unevenly.

Simple rice

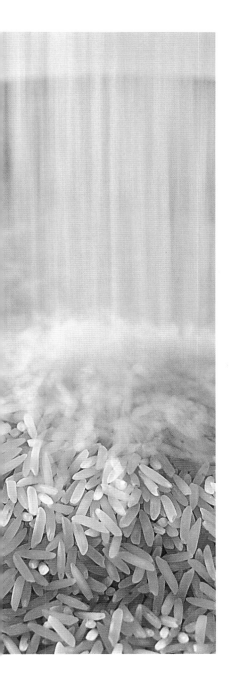

The following recipe is one of the quickest ways to cook rice.

Serves 2 to 4

White Basmati rice (300ml level in a measuring jug)
325ml water
1 tablespoons olive oil
¼ teaspoon salt or to taste

Wash the rice thoroughly and soak for 30 minutes, then drain.

Meanwhile, in a heavy-bottomed pot, bring the water and salt to the boil. Tip the drained rice into the boiling water. Add the olive oil, mix and bring to the boil again. Reduce the heat to very low, cover and cook for 20 minutes. Note that this timing is only for white *Basmati* rice. Remove from the heat and let it rest, covered, for a further 5 minutes.

Uncover, fluff up with a fork and sprinkle with a little olive oil or butter if desired. Serve hot.

Variation 1: If you want a crispy layer at the bottom, use a non-stick pan and proceed as above. Once the 20 minutes have elapsed, cook for another 15 minutes, on the lowest setting. (You can put a heat diffuser beneath the pot and cook for longer.)

Serve it like a cake by tipping the pan upside down on to a plate. (**Tip:** Put a plate on the top of the pot, hold it firmly down with one hand and turn the pot upside down with the other.)

Variation 2: If you want to colour the rice and give it a subtle taste, mix in one heaped tablespoon of tomato paste in the water before cooking the rice. For a yellow colour, and a slightly smoky flavour, mix in ½ a teaspoon of turmeric instead.

Variation 3: For an aromatic rice, just add 4 pods of cardamom in the boiling water before cooking the rice.

Auntie Eileen's rice

This is my Aunt Eileen's recipe for her famously delectable rice. She makes a huge pot of it every Friday for dinner. Her family take it in turns to host these dinners, but whenever she is the guest she brings her hot pot of rice, covered in wads of newspaper and numerous towels to keep it warm. No Friday night dinner would be the same without her unique and glorious rice.

Serves 6

White Basmati rice (700ml level in a measuring jug)
800ml water
150g vermicelli
90ml vegetable oil
A pinch of curry powder
4 tablespoons tomato paste
1 tablespoon salt or to taste
For the garnish
2 onions, cut in half and finely sliced
A handful of blanched nibbed almonds

Wash the rice and soak for 1 hour and drain.

Meanwhile, spread the almonds on an oven tray and place in a fan-heated oven at 150°C until golden. You can also dry fry them in a frying pan. Set aside.

In a large heavy-bottomed pan, heat the oil and fry the onions with the curry powder. As soon as each onion ring turns golden brown take it out with a slotted spoon and place on a plate lined with kitchen paper to absorb the excess oil. Take out only half the onions in this way and set aside. Leave the rest in the pot.

Now add the raw vermicelli to the fried onions in the pot and stir well. Add the salt, the tomato paste and the water. Stir to mix and bring to the boil.

Add the drained rice. Stir to mix and bring to the boil again. Cover and continue boiling for about 5 minutes.

Then gently mix the rice with a large spoon, folding it over once. Reduce the heat to as low as possible. Cover tightly (make sure that your cover is tight-fitting) and cook for 25 minutes.

You can **either** serve the rice straight away **or,** continue to cook on the lowest setting for a further 15 to 20 minutes to ensure the formation of a toasted crust at the bottom. (At this point, you can place a heat diffuser beneath the pan.)

Alternatively, put the pot in the oven, preheated to 100°C/Gas Mark ¼ and leave to cook for 30 minutes or more until ready to serve.

Serve on a platter with the toasted rice on top. Decorate with the reserved fried onions and slivers of almonds.

Rice with red lentils

Kichree

This is the Iraqi version of the Indian *Kichree* dish: rice cooked with red lentils. Thursday was *kichree* day for most Babylonian Jewish households, in Baghdad. It was the only vegetarian dish of the week. The traditional recipe includes cumin in its ingredients. If you find the taste too strong, halve the amount of cumin.

Serves 2 to 4

White Basmati rice (400ml level in a measuring jug)
150ml red lentils
450ml water
3 tablespoons olive or vegetable oil
1 small onion, finely chopped
3 cloves garlic, finely chopped
1½ teaspoons ground cumin
3 tablespoons tomato purée
Salt to taste

Wash the rice and soak for 30 minutes. Wash the lentils and combine with the rice and soak for a further 10 minutes.

Meanwhile, in a large pan, fry the onion in a little oil until golden.

Add the garlic and stir-fry for a few seconds, taking care not to allow the garlic to burn. Remove the pan from the heat. Add the cumin and mix well. Then add the water, the 3 tablespoons of oil, the tomato purée and the salt. Return to the heat and bring to the boil.

Add the drained rice and lentils and bring back to the boil. Cover and cook on low heat for 25 minutes. Take off the heat and let it rest for 10 minutes before serving.

Serve hot with yoghurt or fried eggs, sunny side up. You can also garnish with crispy fried onion rings and melted *haloumi* cheese.

Onion rice
Timman w'basal

The caramelised onions give the rice a wonderful taste and colour.

Serves 5 to 6

White Basmati rice (600ml level in a measuring jug)
650ml water
½ teaspoon vegetable cube or *Bouillon* powder
1 large onion, halved and thinly sliced
3 tablespoons olive oil
1 level teaspoon turmeric
Salt and pepper to taste

Wash the rice and soak for 30 minutes and drain.

Heat the olive oil in a non-stick pot and gently fry the onions until they become dark brown and caramelised (but not burnt).

Add the water and vegetable stock and stir. The water will become brown.

Now add the drained rice to the water and bring to the boil. Continue boiling half-covered on medium heat for about 4 minutes. Then reduce the heat to the lowest setting, cover and cook for 20 minutes. Uncover, gently fluff up the rice and sprinkle with a little olive oil. Cover and cook for another 10 minutes.

You can **either** serve the rice straight away **or,** continue to cook on the lowest setting, for a further 15 to 20 minutes to ensure the formation of a toasted crust at the bottom. (At this point, you can place a heat diffuser beneath the pan.)

To serve as a cake, turn the pot upside down on a plate.
(**Tip:** Put a plate on the top of the pot, hold it firmly down with one hand and turn the pot upside down with the other.)

Yellow mushroom rice

Timman asfar b'kemme

This is a great rice dish which was originally cooked with *Kemme*, the Iraqi Desert Truffles. These are available in tins in most Middle Eastern shops. However, I prefer to use fresh chestnut mushrooms instead, which give a similar earthy flavour.

Serves 4

White Basmati rice (400ml level in a measuring jug)
450ml water
1 large onion, finely chopped
250g chestnut mushrooms, thinly sliced
1 tablespoon vegetable cube or Bouillon powder.
2 tablespoons olive oil
½ teaspoon turmeric

Wash the rice and soak for 30 minutes, then drain.

In a non-stick saucepan fry the onions in a little olive oil, stirring occasionally. When they turn golden brown add the sliced mushrooms, the bouillon powder and the turmeric. Stir and cook until the mushrooms soften.

Pour the water over the mushrooms, stir well and bring to the boil. Add the drained rice and the olive oil and bring to the boil again. Reduce the heat to low cover and cook for 25 minutes.

If you want a crust at the bottom, lower the heat to the lowest setting or place a diffuser underneath the pot and continue cooking for another 15 minutes.

To serve as a cake turn the pot upside down on a plate.
Tip: Put a plate on the top of the pot, hold it firmly down with one hand and turn the pot upside down with the other.

Desert truffles

Kemme

We call these desert truffles *kemme* or *chemma*; also called 'Daughters of Thunder', in Arabic, because they multiply rapidly when thunder occurs. Much like a potato in shape but very uneven and more knobbly, *kemme* can be white, black or brown and grow to the size of an orange or a walnut. All truffles are subterranean plants. Like mushrooms, they are collected in the early morning when the dew is still present and the ground is humid. Some grow in forests and are found in Europe; others grow in the arid regions of North Africa and the Middle East. Libya and Iraq, in particular, are famed for their desert truffles. The Iraqi ones have a stronger smoky taste.

During the 1970s in Iraq people did not eat meat for about 4 months, due to an epidemic which affected numerous herds of sheep. Fortunately for them truffles grew abundantly that year due to unstable weather conditions and they used the fungi as a meat substitute, cooking it with the usual vegetables in the various traditional sauces.

Desert truffles are nowhere near as expensive as the European Forest truffles which can fetch up to £3000 per kilo today.

My husband Frank and I had the pleasure of eating some recently. Back from his travels in the Gulf, a friend of ours brought a huge quantity of Desert truffles with him. He generously gave us two kilos. They had the appearance of small dirty stones. I washed them thoroughly and peeled them; then I boiled some, cooked some with rice, and added a handful to a bowl of pasta. The taste was like that of a strong mushroom.

Meat

Meat

We did not eat beef in Baghdad, only lamb and chicken. Lamb was by far the favourite meat in Iraq where the sheep are quite lean, except for their tails which hung heavy with their fat – unlike British sheep which have fat spread all over their body. As children we used to fight over the barbecued pieces of fat that came skewered with cubes of lamb and onions; we preferred them to the meat!

Beef, and sometimes chicken, can be substituted for lamb in most of the following recipes.

Kebab

Shefta

Traditionally, minced lamb is used for this recipe but you can, also, use minced beef or a mixture of both.

Makes 8 short kebabs

300g minced beef or lamb
1 large onion, finely grated or chopped
6 tablespoons finely chopped flat parsley

The seasoning
½ teaspoon of turmeric
1 garlic clove, crushed
2 tablespoons olive oil
¼ teaspoon cayenne pepper
½ teaspoon ground cumin
½ teaspoon paprika or Baharat p.24
1 tablespoon salt or to taste

Combine all the ingredients in a bowl, mix and knead well with your hands. Cover and let the meat rest for an hour in the refrigerator.

Meanwhile, turn the grill to its highest setting and lightly oil a baking tray.

Divide the meat into tangerine-sized balls. Skewer the meatballs and gently squeeze to elongate their shape. The meat should hug the skewer firmly.

Place the skewers on the tray and grill, for about 5 minutes on each side or until the meat has browned.

Before serving, sprinkle some za'atar and ground cumin on the kebabs, this really makes a difference. Serve hot with warm pitta bread, sliced tomatoes, sliced onions sprinkled with *sumac*, and some pickles.

Kubba

Iraqis call it *kubba*, the Lebanese and Syrians *kibbeh*, the Egyptians *kobeba* and in Jerusalem it is *kubba*. All Middle Eastern countries make *kubba* dishes.

What is *kubba*? From the Arabic meaning ball, *kubba* is basically a meatball, or a meat filling, covered with a layer of rice, *burghul* (cracked wheat) or potato. A meat ball without a cover is not a *kubba*, it remains a naked meatball!

Many shapes of *kubba* abound, with as many recipes. We have small round *kubba*s cooked in a sweet and sour sauce, flat *kubba*s of different sizes either baked or boiled, and oval ones which are fried. *Kubba* dishes vary slightly from country to country, with each community bringing its own subtle variation on the theme.

Baked wheat *kubba* in a tray

Kubba burghul b'siniya

This is such a tasty dish; a spicy meat filling, sandwiched between a shell of two layers of *burghul* wheat. (*Burghul* is wheat that has been hulled, parboiled then dried and ground. You can buy 3 different grades: coarse, medium and fine. A mixture of medium and fine is used for this *kubba dish*.

It might appear fiddly at first but it is easy to make. My nephew, Jesse, loved it so much that he asked me to teach him how to make it. We had a great time cooking together and eating the fruits of our endeavour.

I recommend laying out the ingredients for the shell and the filling separately. The meat filling should be prepared first, followed by the *burghul* shell.

Serves 6

In all you will need
850g finely minced lean beef
or lamb

The burghul shell (upper and
lower)
300g mixture of medium and
fine *burghul* wheat
350g minced lean beef or lamb
2 tablespoons olive oil
1 teaspoon cinnamon
Salt and pepper to taste

The filling
2 medium onions, finely
chopped
500g minced lamb
Juice of ½ lemon
2 tablespoons chopped
sultanas
1 tablespoon allspice
1 teaspoon ground turmeric
1 teaspoon ground cinnamon
70g pine nuts
Salt and pepper to taste

Making the filling

Sauté the onions in a little olive oil until golden brown. Add the minced lamb and cook on medium heat, stirring from time to time, dispersing all the lumps. Do this until the meat is cooked and all the water has evaporated. Add the lemon juice, spices, salt, pepper and pine nuts. Mix well while cooking for another minute. Remove from the heat and set aside.

Preheat the oven to 200°C/Gas Mark 6

Making the *burghul* shell (upper and lower)

Wash the *burghul* thoroughly in cold water and let it soak in a bowl for 10 minutes. Then take a small handful at a time and squeeze out the water, placing the squeezed *burghul* in another bowl. Add the 300g meat, cinnamon, olive oil and salt and pepper. Wet your hands and knead into a soft dough.

Either continue to knead until smooth, remembering to wet your hands to avoid the dough from sticking to them, **or** transfer the mixture to a blender, add a tablespoon of water (if too dry) and mix to obtain a smooth paste. Divide the dough into 2 equal parts and set aside.

Lightly grease an ovenproof dish (about 30 by 20cm) with olive oil. With wet hands, spread one-half of the dough in the dish and flatten evenly to the edges. Brush the top of the flattened dough with a little olive oil.

Spread the meat filling evenly over the dough.

Covering the meat filling with the other half of the dough is a little tricky. Spread a sheet of cling film (twice the size of the ovenproof dish) on a pastry board or work surface. Place the *burghul* dough in the middle of the sheet and lightly flatten it with your palm. Brush the surface with a little olive oil. Place another sheet of cling film of the same size on top of the dough. With a rolling pin gently roll the dough to about the size and shape of the ovenproof dish. Peel back

the top layer of cling film. Slide the palm of one hand underneath the bottom layer of cling film and flip the dough on to the meat filling and peel off the cling film. Now, with wet hands, pat the dough down all over, especially around the edges and with a wet knife, cut around the edges to prevent it from sticking to the dish.

With a wet knife, score a diagonal line from one corner to the other. Continue to make parallel lines, about 5cm apart. Do the same from the opposite side to obtain diamond shaped portions and a pleasant design.

Mix 2 tablespoons of olive oil with 2 tablespoons water. Brush the crust generously with this mixture. Bake in the preheated oven for 50 minutes. Thereafter, brush the crust with some olive oil and place under the grill until it becomes crisp and toasted.

Serve hot, in the oven dish, with a tomato and flat parsley salad.

Potato *Kubba*

Kubba patayta

A tasty and spicy meat filling is wrapped in a layer of mashed potatoes and then fried to a golden colour. This is the traditional way of cooking them. I tried brushing them with olive oil and baking them instead, but the taste was not authentic. When time is short, I arrange the filling in an oven proof dish, spread the mashed potato on top and bake in the oven. This method makes an easy and quick dinner.

Makes about 15

The Shell
900g potatoes (choose ones that do not collapse when cooked)
2 to 3 tablespoons oil for frying
Bread crumbs
Salt and pepper to taste

The Filling
250g minced meat
1 onion, finely chopped
½ tablespoon curry powder
2 tablespoons sultanas, finely chopped (optional)
A pinch allspice
Salt and pepper to taste
1 teaspoon olive oil
3 tablespoons parsley, finely chopped
1 tablespoon flaked almonds

Boil the potatoes until just soft. Mash them while they are hot and leave to cool. Do not add any water. Add the olive oil, salt and pepper. Wet your hands and knead well; you should have a stiff consistency.

In a large frying pan, heat a little oil and sauté the chopped onions until soft. Stir in the curry, the allspice and the sultanas, if using. Add the meat, salt and pepper and stir-fry until the meat is cooked and all the water has evaporated. Make sure to flatten the lumps. Stir in the almond flakes and cook for a minute. Take off the heat, add the chopped parsley, mix and set aside.

Making the *kubba*

Wet your hands and take slightly less than a tennis ball-sized portion of the mashed potatoes. Roll it and flatten it a little in the palm of your hand. Place a tablespoon of the filling in the centre. Keeping your hands moist, bring the sides up over the stuffing and seal. Once completely covered, roll into a ball, brush with the egg and gently roll over the breadcrumbs. Lightly flatten to the shape of a burger. Arrange on a plate, cover with cling film and set aside for 30 minutes in the refrigerator.

In a large saucepan heat a little oil and fry the *kubba* until golden on both sides.

Serve hot with a refreshing tomato or cucumber salad.

Variation 1: Instead of a meat filling you can use soya mince or Quorn.

Variation 2: You can also make a vegetable filling.

Heat a little oil in a frying pan and stir-fry one chopped onion and 2 chopped celery stalks , both very finely chopped. Add 150g mushrooms, very finely chopped (some people use tinned mushrooms) and 1 very finely grated carrot. Add 1 tablespoon tomato paste and 1 teaspoon curry powder, ½ teaspoon turmeric, salt and pepper to taste. Mix and keep stirring on medium heat for a five minutes. Finally, add 1 tablespoon finely chopped parsley. Cover and simmer on low heat for another 20 minutes. Add a little water if too dry. Taste and adjust the seasoning. Take off the heat and set aside to cool.

Proceed to make the potato *kubba* as the main recipe.

Meat Balls and Okra Stew

Kufta w'bamia hameth

The traditional 'Kubba Bamia' dish consists of meat balls wrapped in a thin rice shell stewed in a sweet and sour sauce with okra. To make it a less time consuming dish whilst preserving the integrity of the flavours, just roll the mince meat into small balls (no rice casing) and simmer with the okra vegetables in a sweet and sour tomato sauce.

Serves 4

400g frozen okra

The Meat Balls
250g minced beef or lamb
4 tablespoons finely chopped
    flat parsley
Salt and pepper to taste

The Sauce
1 onion, finely chopped
1 tablespoon of olive oil
2 large fresh tomatoes, finely
    chopped
1 tablespoon tomato paste
2 lemons, juiced
1 litre water
1 to 2 tablespoons sugar
½ teaspoon stock or Swiss
    Bouillon powder
Salt and pepper to taste

To make the meat balls, mix the mince meat and parsley and season with salt and pepper. Mix well into a smooth paste. Wet your hands and roll the mixture into small balls the size of a large cherry or a small walnut. Place on a tray.

Take a large saucepan (wide enough to cook the meat balls without overcrowding them) and sauté the chopped onion in a little oil until soft and golden. Stir in the chopped tomatoes and simmer until they melt. Add the meat balls, cover and cook for 15 minutes. Shake the pan from time to time so that they will cook evenly.

Add the tomato paste, stock powder, salt and pepper, and enough hot water to cover the meat balls. Bring to the boil, cook covered on medium heat for about 20 minutes, stirring occasionally.

Add the frozen okra and bring back to the boil, adding more water if the sauce has dried up. Turn the heat down a little and cook until the okra is done.

Mix the sugar and lemon juice and pour in. Taste and adjust the flavour of the sauce. Simmer for a few more minutes until the sauce thickens a little.

Serve hot with plain or turmeric rice.

Beetroot *Kubba* Stew

Kubba Shwandar

Serves 6 to 8

You will need, in all, 450g finely minced lean beef or lamb

8 to 10 uncooked medium beetroots

The Filling
325g minced lamb
4 tablespoons finely chopped flat parsley
Salt and pepper

The Shell
250g fine ground rice
125g minced lamb
Salt and pepper

The Sauce
1 onion finely chopped
1 tablespoon of olive oil
1 heaped tablespoon tomato paste
3 lemons, juiced
1 litre water
1 tablespoon sugar
Salt and pepper to taste

This is one of our favourite traditional dishes. Consisting of meat balls wrapped in a thin rice casing and cooked with beetroots in a sweet and sour sauce.

Preheat the oven to 190°C/Gas Mark 5. Wash the beetroots, wrap them in foil and bake for 1 hour.

Making the filling

Mix the filling ingredients together and set aside.

Making the shell

Prepare a bowl of cold water.

Place the shell ingredients with 2 to 3 tablespoons of water in a blender to obtain a smooth, but firm paste. Wet your palms and roll the mixture into balls about the size of a small walnut and set aside.

Flatten each ball as thinly as you can, placing a teaspoon of the filling in the centre. Gently gather up the sides of the dough to cover the filling, delicately pinch it closed, and roll into a ball. Arrange on a tray and set aside.

To make the sauce

Take a large saucepan, wide enough to cook the *kubba* balls without overcrowding them. Sauté the chopped onion in the olive oil on medium heat until soft and golden.

Add the chopped tomatoes. Cover and simmer on a low heat for about 15 minutes, stirring occasionally.

Add the tomato paste, water, salt and pepper, and bring to the boil.

Carefully lower the *kubba balls,* one at a time, into the sauce. This is critical, as any jarring will cause them to open up or break. The liquid should cover the *kubba* completely. If not, add water. Reduce the heat to a gentle simmer and cook for about 25 minutes. (Remember that the *kubba* are extremely fragile so should not be disturbed whilst cooking.)

Unwrap the baked beetroots; set aside to cool enough to handle. Peel off the skin and slice them or cut them into cubes. Gently drop the beetroot into the pot.

Mix the sugar and lemon juice and pour in. Taste and adjust the flavour of the sauce. Cover and simmer for another 20 minutes until you have a slightly thickened sauce.

Variation: A much quicker way to make this dish would be to leave out the shell and the raw beetroots. Just make it with meat balls and ready-cooked beetroots and proceed as above. This variation cuts preparation time in half and the taste is great too.

Rice patties with meat and dried lime

Uruq b'ruz

Makes about 20 patties

**You will need, in all,
700g finely lean lamb or beef**

The Shell
400g lean minced lamb or
   beef
600g Basmati rice
½ teaspoon salt and
½ pepper or to taste

The Filling
300g lean minced lamb or
   beef
2 onions, finely chopped
5 dried limes, pulverised
   (5 heaped tablespoons)
Salt and pepper to taste

The pulverised dried lime, mixed with the meat, gives this dish a delectable flavour. Dried limes (*noumi Basra*) are available from most Iranian or Middle Eastern shops. They should be purchased whole and ground as needed, otherwise the flavour evaporates. Cut open with a knife, take out the pips and pulverise to a fine powder in a coffee grinder or mortar and pestle.

I recommend that you prepare all the ingredients first. It will make the procedure much easier as preparation takes a little time but the making of the patties is easy and most enjoyable.

Wash the rice and soak for half an hour, then drain.

Making the filling

Mix the meat with the onions, ground limes, salt and pepper.

Making the shell

Prepare a bowl of cold water.

Wet your hands and knead the meat into a smooth paste. Set aside.

Take a small portion of meat at a time, gently mix it with as much rice as it can hold, and set aside. Repeat this until you have mixed all the meat with all the rice. Pack all the meat into one lump and place in a bowl. Sprinkle a little water on the mixture. Cover and let it rest in the refrigerator for one hour.

Making the patties

Wet your palms and take a tangerine-sized portion of the shell mixture and carefully flatten it on your palm.

Place a heaped tablespoon of the filling in the centre. Keeping your hands moist, bring the sides up over the stuffing and seal. Then flatten it slightly and place on a tray.

To cook

You will be cooking the patties in two or three batches, depending on the size of your saucepan. You will be aiming to put 7 to 8 patties in each pan. Remember, the rice will double in size so it is important not to overcrowd them.

Half fill the saucepan with water or stock. Add half a tablespoon of salt and bring to the boil.

Slowly lower the patties, one by one, into the boiling water making sure that all of them are submerged. Bring back to the boil. Then turn down the heat a little and cook, half covered, until the patties begin to float to the top – about 20 to 25 minutes.

Remove with a slotted spoon, drain and place on a dish.

You can serve them straightaway, in a soup bowl with a ladle or two of the stock poured over them, or drizzled with a some olive oil and accompanied by some steamed vegetables.

In keeping with tradition, allow them to cool and then fry them in a little olive oil or brush them with oil and bake in the oven at 190°C/Gas Mark 5 for 20 minutes or until crisp. Alternatively, you can freeze them, cooked or uncooked, for use at a later date.

Sweet and sour pumpkin and meat stew

Qagh'e ahmar hameth

This was a traditional sweet and sour dish that we used to eat throughout the winter months, in Baghdad. I sometimes make it with butternut squash and that works very well too. I have added some prunes, fresh ginger and orange zest to deepen the flavours. This dish is even tastier if cooked a few hours before eating it, giving the flavours time to mingle and intensify. So I cook it in the morning to serve it for dinner.

Gently fry the onion, garlic and ginger on a low heat until soft.

Add the meat and then turn the heat up to high and stir to seal on all sides. Add the tinned tomatoes, cook until all the juices evaporate.

Add enough water to cover the meat and bring to the boil. Cover and lower the heat to medium. Cook for 45 minutes or until the meat is tender. Ensure that the water does not dry out, adding small quantities of hot water as necessary.

Add orange zest, sultanas, prunes, salt and sugar. Stir to mix and bring to the boil. Add the bite-sized cubes of squash, lower the heat to medium and cook for a further 15 minutes. Add the lemon juice. At this point, taste and adjust the flavour of the sauce to your liking. If you find it too lemony, add a bit more sugar and vice versa.

Cover and continue to cook for 15 minutes or so. Watch the sauce does not boil away, adding small quantities of hot water as necessary, until you have a slightly thickened sauce.

Serve hot with rice or mash potatoes.

Serves 4 to 5

500g lamb or beef, cubed
700g pumpkin or butternut
   squash, peeled and cubed
3 heaped tablespoons
   sultanas
7 prunes, coarsely chopped
1 piece fresh ginger 5cm long,
   finely chopped
400ml tinned tomatoes,
   chopped
1 onion, coarsely chopped
1 garlic clove, coarsely
   chopped
3 lemons, juiced
zest of 2 oranges
3 tablespoons sugar or agave
2 tablespoon olive oil
1½ teaspoon salt or to taste

Sweet and sour aubergine and lamb stew

Ingiryie

Serves 4 to 6

500g lamb or beef, cubed
1 small onion, finely chopped
2 aubergines
3 red peppers, thinly sliced
3 medium sized tomatoes,
   sliced in round discs
3 onions, thinly sliced in rings
8 pitted prunes
Olive oil
½ tablespoon curry powder
Salt and pepper

The sauce

3 tablespoons tomato paste
2 tablespoons sugar or agave
2½ lemons, juiced
A pinch of cayenne pepper
Salt and pepper to taste

The aubergine or eggplant, as it is sometimes called, comes in different colours and sizes. Pear-shaped, squat or round, small or large, its colour varies from dark purple and green to striated and white. It is in India, where the eggplant first originated, that one can find most of these varieties. The seeds of the larger and older aubergines are brown and bitter. The method of salting aubergine before cooking is recommended prior to frying, as it draws out the moisture and with it most of the bitterness. Called 'dergorging', this method also helps to reduce its capacity for absorbing too much oil. You do not need to degorge if you are not intending to fry them.

Slice the aubergine into round discs about 2cm thick. Place in a colander. Salt liberally, making sure all the slices are covered, and leave for 30 minutes.

Soak the prunes in cold water.

Meanwhile, heat a tablespoon of olive oil in a saucepan and sauté the chopped onion on medium heat until limp. Season the meat with the curry powder, salt and pepper, and add to the onions. Sauté until the meat is browned and the water has evaporated. Add about 100ml boiling water and cook covered over a low heat for at least an hour or until the meat is meltingly soft. You want the meat to cook in its own juices, but keep an eye on the water level, adding a little more water when it dries up.

Preheat the oven to 180°C/Gas Mark 4.

Thoroughly rinse the aubergines and pat dry with some kitchen paper. Pan-fry, on both sides, with a little olive oil. Set aside. Next, stir-fry the onion rings, then the peppers, until soft and set aside separately.

Lightly oil an oven dish and arrange all the meat at the bottom. Place a single layer of aubergine on top followed by the onions, prunes and peppers. Top this with another layer of aubergine. Finish with a layer of the sliced tomatoes.

Mix all the sauce ingredients until the sugar has dissolved. It should taste a little lemony to lift the flavour of the dish. Taste and adjust the seasoning. Pour over the dish and bake in the oven for about 50 minutes.

Serve hot with some rice. All stews are tastier the next day, when flavours have had time to intensify. This one is no exception and it is also delicious eaten cold.

Variation: Instead of frying, I grill the aubergine and pepper rings, brushed with a little olive oil. As a further variation, I sometimes like to char the skin of the peppers and remove it. This imparts a smoky flavour which I love. Removing the skin also makes for a softer texture. To do this, grill the peppers whole until the skin is black and charred, immediately pop them in a plastic bag, seal and leave them for a few minutes. This makes it very easy to peel away the charred skin.

Skewered marinated lamb

Laham meshwi

Serves 3 to 4

500g lamb or beef, cubed
2 large onions, cut into
   quarters
1 or 2 red peppers, seeded
   and cut into chunks

The Marinade:
2 garlic cloves, crushed
1 teaspoon grated ginger
½ tablespoon curry powder
1 teaspoon turmeric
¼ teaspoon cayenne pepper
3 tablespoons olive oil
2 lemons, juiced
½ teaspoon *sumac* (p.25)
   (optional)
Salt to taste

This is a simple recipe that is very big on flavour. The longer you marinate the meat the softer it becomes. Lamb is usually used but beef can be substituted. You can serve it with rice or mashed potatoes, or eat it in a pitta bread, stuffed with pickles and fresh tomatoes. The marinade can also be used for small lamb chops or chicken pieces before grilling or barbecuing.

Combine the marinade ingredients in a bowl. Tip the meat into the marinade and mix well to coat all the pieces. Cover and leave in the refrigerator for at least an hour or overnight.

Thread the meat on the skewers, alternating with the peppers and the onion pieces. Place under the grill until the meat is cooked on all sides, turning once.

Serve with a tomato salad, turshi pickles (p.161) and pitta bread.

Real Beef Burgers

Our household is famous for its beef burgers. I mention *'bharat'* (p.24) in the ingredients. This is a mixture of ground spices that you can buy from leading supermarket chains. Failing that, you can use allspice or mixed spice.

500g sirloin steak, minced twice
2 large onions, finely chopped
3 heaped tablespoons flat parsley, finely chopped
1 teaspoon turmeric
1 teaspoon ground paprika
A pinch of cayenne pepper
2 tablespoons of olive oil
½ teaspoon of bharat or allspice
Salt and pepper to taste

Fry the onions until soft and golden. Set aside to cool.

Then combine the onions with the rest of the ingredients in a bowl. Mix and knead well with your hands. Cover and let the meat rest for an hour in the refrigerator, the longer the better.

Prepare a bowl of cold water. Wet your hands, take a portion of meat the size of a small tangerine and roll it softly between your palms to make a ball. You want the burger to be light and airy, so do not press hard as this will make the burger too compact when cooked. Press it gently to flatten it in the shape of a burger. Do this with all the meat.

With a kitchen towel, lightly wipe a non-stick pan with some oil. Place a few burgers at a time in the pan and cook on high heat until one side is golden brown but not burnt. Turn and cook the other side, lightly pressing down the burgers, every so often, with a spatula. Taste one to see if the meat is cooked to your liking.

Variation: You can also barbecue the meat.

Stuffed vegetables

Mahasha

Mehshi means 'stuffed' in Arabic. *Dolma*, a word you are probably more familiar with, is the Turkish equivalent but we use the term *dolma* to designate the stuffed vine leaves only. All sorts of vegetables can be stuffed including onions, tomatoes, courgettes, carrots, aubergines and peppers. The stuffing can be made with meat only, with meat and rice or with a vegetarian mixture.

You may want to begin by stuffing one kind of vegetable only, before moving on to the mixed vegetable platter p.122. The most popular stuffed vegetables in our household are onions, courgettes, aubergines and vine leaves.

One thing to remember: as rice expands when cooked, you must allow for this by loosely stuffing all your vegetables.

Stuffed courgettes

Kousa mahasha

Serves 4

8 courgettes

The Stuffing

225g minced lamb

1 onion, finely chopped

5 tablespoons finely chopped
fresh mint

3 tablespoon finely chopped
flat parsley

1 tablespoon olive oil

Salt and pepper to taste

The Sauce

2 large tomatoes, finely
chopped

5 tablespoons finely chopped
fresh mint

1 garlic clove, finely chopped

1 bay leaf

200ml water

1½ to 2 lemons, juiced

1 tablespoon of sugar

Variation: Instead of the meat
you can use soya mince with
chopped chestnut mushrooms.

Wash, top and tail the courgettes. Cut in half to end up with 16 cylindrical pieces. Using a corer, or peeler, scoop out the centre. Do not cut right through. Leave one end closed. Set aside the cored courgettes and the scooped out flesh.

The sauce

In a deep frying pan, or saucepan, large enough to hold all the stuffed courgettes in a single layer, combine the scooped out flesh with the sauce ingredients, except for the sugar and lemon juice. Bring to the boil, then simmer for 15 minutes.

Meanwhile, mix the stuffing ingredients and loosely stuff the courgettes, smoothing off the tops.

Arrange the vegetables in the simmering sauce, adding more hot water if necessary to half cover them. Turn the heat up and boil for 2 minutes. Then reduce to a simmer, cover and cook for 15 to 20 minutes.

Mix the sugar with the lemon juice and pour over the courgettes. Taste and adjust the sweet and sour flavour to your liking. Cover and simmer for a further 10 minutes or so. Take off the heat and let it rest for a few minutes. Serve hot with rice.

Stuffed aubergines
Sheikh mehshi

Serves 4 to 6

4 aubergines on the slim side

The Stuffing
300g lean minced lamb
2 to 3 celery stalks, finely chopped
½ lemon, juiced
1 teaspoon tomato paste
2 onions, finely chopped
4 tablespoons flat parsley, finely chopped
1 tablespoon fresh mint, finely chopped
½ teaspoon olive oil

The Sauce
3½ lemons, juiced
400g fresh or canned tomatoes, chopped
1 tablespoon tomato paste
2 teaspoons sugar
Salt and pepper to taste

This is one of my mother's specialities, a sweet and sour dish which brings out the flavours of the aubergines. Usually the vegetable is stuffed whole. The recipe below, however, calls for it to be cut sideways so as to open up like a concertina. The stuffing is then placed between the slices. Lamb is the favoured meat, but you can substitute it with beef or soya mince.

Wash and cut the tops of the aubergine. Lay them on their sides and cut slices across the width about 1cm thick. Do not slice right through, the disks must remain attached at the bottom.

Prepare a bowl of cold water near you. Combine all the stuffing ingredients in another bowl. Wet your hands and knead well.

Stuff the mixture between the slices of aubergine. You will notice that the aubergines will fan out. Carefully lay them in a suitably sized saucepan, in a single layer, so that the slices hold firmly together.

Mix all the sauce ingredients, making sure that the sugar dissolves. Taste and adjust the seasoning. Pour over the aubergines.

Bring to the boil, then lower the heat to medium simmer, cover and cook for 30 minutes or until the aubergines look slightly wrinkled and the sauce has thickened. (Watch that the sauce does not dry up. Top up with water if necessary whilst cooking.)

Variation: As a decoration, you can peel the skin of the aubergine in alternate stripes lengthways before cutting them into disks.

Stuffed mixed vegetable platter

Mahasha

Serves 4 to 5

Vegetables to stuff
1 very small red pepper or
   2 small tomatoes
2 courgettes
2 to 3 onions
12 or more vine leaves

The stuffing
250g rice
250g minced lamb
1 tablespoon olive oil
2½ tablespoons tomato paste
1 large fresh tomato,
   chopped and peeled
6 heaped tablespoons finely
   chopped flat parsley
5 tablespoons finely
   chopped mint
The segments of 2 large
   lemons
¾ teaspoon salt
A pinch of pepper

The stewing liquid
4 tablespoons lemon juice
4 tablespoons sugar
3 tablespoons tomato paste
2 garlic cloves, peeled and
   chopped
1 teaspoon salt

This recipe was given to me by my Aunt Doreen who makes a most delicious *mahasha*. Traditionally, the *dolma* is made with fresh vine leaves; if you can't get hold of some, the alternative is to buy them vacuume-packed in jars from Middle Eastern shops.

For this recipe, I would recommend preparing all the ingredients in 3 lots, before starting to cook.

Wash the rice and soak for 30 minutes or so.

The stewing liquid

Combine all the stewing liquid ingredients, making sure the sugar dissolves, and set aside.

The vegetables

Peel the onions. Slit one side of each onion from top to bottom. Cut only half way through. Boil them for 10 to 15 minutes until the layers can be detached and separated. Drain and leave to cool.

Meanwhile, wash the pepper (or tomatoes), slice off its top and reserve as it will be used as a cover. (You do the same for the tomatoes.) Remove the core and seeds.

Wash the courgettes. Peel them and cut in half. Core them three-quarters of the way and reserve the inside. This will be added to the stuffing.

Now, wash the vine leaves and soak them in boiling water for two to three minutes. Unravel the cooled onion skins. These will be filled with the stuffing.

The Stuffing

With a sharp knife cut away the peel and the pith of the 2 lemons. Carefully cut out all the segments and slice them in small pieces.

Drain the rice and tip it into a bowl. Add the minced meat, a little at a time and knead well. Add the cored bits of courgettes and the rest of the stuffing ingredients and mix well.

Prepare a deep frying pan or saucepan, large enough to hold all the stuffed vegetables in a single layer, and coat the bottom with 2 tablespoons of oil.

Stuff each onion skin with a tablespoon of stuffing, close and arrange tightly in the pan. Stuff the courgettes and arrange next to the onions. Stuff the pepper, cover it with its sliced top and put it in the middle of the pan.

Now, take a vine leaf. Place a tablespoon of stuffing in the middle, fold and roll once, tuck in the edges and roll till the end. Arrange each stuffed vine leaf tightly one next to the other. If there is no room at the bottom of the pan put the vine leaves on top of the other vegetables.

Cook the vegetables on low heat for about 3 minutes, then, pour the stewing liquid over them, covering them three-quarters of the way up. Bring to the boil and continue cooking, half-covered, for 5 minutes.

Reduce the heat to medium, cover and cook for 30 minutes.

Reduce the heat to a simmer and cook covered for another 50 minutes or until almost all the liquid has been absorbed, leaving very little sauce at the bottom of the pot. Add more water whilst cooking, if necessary. Be careful not to burn the vegetables.

Serve on a platter with the pepper or tomatoes in the middle.

Variation: You can substitute fine soya mince for the meat.

Vegetarian *dolma*

Dolma b'mkhadar

This refreshing vegetarian dish is popular as a finger
snack or a light meal, served hot or cold. If you can't
get hold of fresh vine leaves, the alternative is to buy
them packed in jars from Middle Eastern shops.

20 to 30 vine leaves

The stuffing
1 kg fresh tomatoes, finely chopped
3 onions, finely chopped
500g rice
The flesh of 2 lemons, coarsely chopped
A big bunch of parsley, finely chopped
A small bunch of mint, finely chopped
400ml chopped tinned tomatoes
1 tablespoon sugar
130ml olive oil

The stewing liquid
3 tablespoons lemon juice
3 tablespoons sugar
3 tablespoons tomato paste
1 garlic clove, peeled and chopped
1 teaspoon salt

Combine all the stuffing ingredients in a big bowl and mix well.

Wash the vine leaves and soak them in boiling water for two minutes.

Line a large and deep saucepan with 2 layers of thin slices of lemon. The lemon will prevent the leaves from burning or drying out whilst cooking, giving them a lemony edge.

Take a vine leaf, smooth side down, and place a tablespoon of stuffing in the middle. Fold and roll once, tuck in the edges and roll till the end. Arrange the stuffed vine leaves in the saucepan, on top of the lemon slices. They should be placed as close together as possible.

Combine all ingredients for the stewing liquid, making sure the sugar dissolves. Pour liquid over the vine leaves, covering them completely. Add more water, if necessary. Bring to the boil and continue cooking, half-covered, for 5 minutes.

Reduce the heat to medium, cover and cook for a 30 minutes. At this point, taste and adjust the sweet and sour sauce to your liking by adding more lemon or more sugar.

Reduce the heat to a simmer and cook covered for another hour, or until almost all the liquid has been absorbed, leaving very little sauce at the bottom of the pot. Add more water whilst cooking, if needed.

Serve as a light meal with a salad or part of a *mezze* spread.

Egg and meat fritters

Beith b'Laham

This is a light dish which is very popular with my family. The traditional recipe calls for fried meat fritters but, to save time, you can cook it as one large omelette or tortilla, and slice it as a cake when serving. If you are not a meat lover, soya mince can be substituted.

Steam the diced or grated potatoes until soft. This should take about 10 to 15 minutes. Transfer to a dish, season with salt and pepper and set aside to cool.

Season the meat with the cumin, curry powder, salt and pepper and mix in 1 tablespoon of olive oil.

Beat the eggs in a large bowl and mix in the rest of the ingredients. The mixture should be soft but not watery. The eggs act as a binder, holding all the ingredients together. You can add another egg if necessary.

In a large frying pan, heat 2 tablespoons of oil. Drop a tablespoonful of the mixture into the hot oil, lower the heat to medium-low and lightly flatten the mixture with the back of a spoon. Cook each side until golden brown. Cook in batches, a few at a time, transferring on to kitchen towel to absorb the excess oil.

Serve with a tomato or cucumber salad and some pickles.

Variation 1: You can substitute soya mince instead of the meat. There is a brand called Quorn which you can use straight from the packet. If that is unavailable use dried soya mince. Soak the soya in water for about 20 minutes. Squeeze out all the water, season, and cook as above.

Variation 2: This is a quicker version which also uses less oil. It can be served hot or cold and cut into triangles like a cake. Heat a little oil in a large frying pan (about 23cm). Pour in the egg mixture and cook covered on medium-low heat until the bottom has set and turned golden brown. Then, place under the grill to cook the top.

Serves 4

250g minced meat or chicken
1 small onion, very finely chopped
5 eggs
2 medium potatoes, finely diced or grated
1 bunch spring onions, very finely chopped
5 tablespoons finely chopped flat parsley
½ teaspoon ground cumin
1 teaspoon curry powder
1 tablespoon olive oil
Sunflower oil for frying
1 teaspoon salt
Pepper to taste

Savoury cigars
Boureg

From the Greek word meaning leaf, filo pastry is paper thin – almost as fragile as gold leaf! It has to be handled with great care because it tears easily. It must be covered with a slightly damp cloth to stay moist as it dries up quickly. There are many brands of filo; some are frozen and need to be totally defrosted before use, others are ready to use. Follow the manufacturer's instructions before starting this recipe.

The beauty of this finger snack is its versatility and it can be made with minced lamb, beef, chicken or cheese. Traditionally, the *boureg* are deep fried (left) but can be baked in the oven, brushed with a little olive oil. The two methods produce very different results in flavour and texture. Either way they are delicious.

Makes 18 pieces

250g minced lamb
1 onion, finely chopped
5 tablespoons finely
    chopped flat parsley
1½ tablespoon olive oil
1 teaspoon paprika or
    curry powder
½ teaspoon *bharat*
    (p.24) or allspice
Salt and pepper to
    taste

Preheat the oven to 190°C/Gas Mark 5.

Mix the meat with the salt, pepper, paprika and allspice or *bharat.*

Sauté the onion until golden. Add the meat and stir-fry on medium heat until cooked. Make sure you disperse all the lumps. Remove from the heat and mix in the flat parsley. Set aside to cool.

Take a sheet of filo pastry and cut it into 4 squares. Take each square and put 1 tablespoon of meat in the corner closest to you. Carefully fold over to just cover the filling. Then roll once, fold the sides in and continue to roll till the end. Dab the end bit with a little water to make it stick.

Arrange the cigars on a lightly oiled baking tray and brush the tops with a little olive oil. Bake them for about 15 to 20 minutes, turning them once when one side turns golden brown.

Serve as a snack with a tomato salad or include them as part of a mezze spread.

Variation: For a vegetarian version, fill the pastry with grated *haloumi* cheese mixed with feta or cheddar and combine with parsley and paprika. Cook in the oven as above.

Fish

Samak

We ate river fish in Baghdad. Very similar to carp, *shabbut* was the favourite for making *masgouf*, the renowned Iraqi barbecued dish. Apart from Fridays, when our family ate fried fish with rice, we did not eat much of it. We were essentially meat eaters. That said, I eat very little meat these days, my preferred meat is now fish! The following recipes such as baked fish in sweet and sour sauce and dried lime fish patties are delicious traditional dishes which I cook on a regular basis.

Baked fish in sweet and sour sauce
Salona

Serves 4 to 6

800g white fish fillets (haddock, sea bass, sea bream)
4 large onions
3 red peppers
2 fresh tomatoes, sliced into thick rings
1 tablespoon paprika
Salt and pepper to taste

The Sauce

3 lemons, juiced
2 tablespoons tomato paste
2 tablespoons sugar or agave
1 tablespoon curry powder
A dash of cayenne pepper
50ml water
1 teaspoon salt
A handful of chopped flat parsley

Mix all the sauce ingredients in a small saucepan and bring to the boil. Simmer gently for about 5 minutes, stirring from time to time. Remove from the heat, add the flat parsley, taste and adjust the seasoning. Set aside.

With the use of a sharp knife or a mandolin, slice the onions into rings and set aside. Do the same with the peppers. Next, stir-fry the onions rings, then the peppers, until soft and set aside.

Cut the fish fillets into large chunks, brush with olive oil and sprinkle with salt and paprika. Place under the grill and cook for 5 minutes.

Lightly oil a heavy-bottomed saucepan and arrange all the fish at the bottom. Layer the onions on top, followed by the peppers and then the tomatoes. Pour the sauce over them, half cover and simmer gently on a low heat until most of the sauce has been absorbed (about 25 minutes). You can bake the dish if you prefer. Preheat the oven to 190°C/Gas Mark 5. Lightly oil an oven dish and arrange the fish and vegetables as above. Pour the sauce over them and bake for about 30 minutes, until most of the sauce has been absorbed.

Layered rice with fish

Pelau b'samak

I have tried four variations of this dish; some omit the dried lime; others prefer to add the fish on top of the rice; some mix it with the rice and one recipe uses tomatoes. The following is the result of tweaking and combining the best elements of all four, plus a little extra something.

Don't be put off by the long instructions, I promise you the dish is very simple to make and you will not regret the effort. There are three components: Fish, rice and the marinade. The fish and the rice are cooked separately, then combined and simmered together in a casserole for 30 minutes.

Serves 4

White Basmati rice (400ml level in a measuring jug)
450ml water or chicken/vegetable stock
1 onion, finely chopped
2 tablespoons olive oil
4 tablespoons coarsely chopped coriander or
    flat parsley
½ teaspoon salt

550g fillets of haddock with the skin on
2 large onions finely sliced into rings for garnish

The Marinade
2 tablespoons olive oil
3 tablespoons lemon juice
2 tablespoons pulverised dried limes (*noumi Basra*)
1 teaspoon turmeric
1 tablespoon curry powder
1 tablespoon salt
A pinch of cayenne pepper

Wash the rice and soak for 30 minutes or so.

Next, pulverise the dried limes. (Dried limes are available from most Iranian or Middle Eastern shops. They should be purchased whole and ground as needed, otherwise the flavour evaporates.) Cut open with a knife, take out the pips and pulverise to a fine powder in a coffee grinder or mortar and pestle.

The marinade

Combine all the dry marinade ingredients in a shallow bowl, large enough to place all the fish in a single layer. Add the lemon juice and stir into a paste. Add three tablespoons of water and stir again. Now stir in the olive oil.

Before marinating the fish, be sure to remove all fish bones from the fillets. Place the fish fillets in the marinade and coat all over. Set aside in the refrigerator for 10 to 15 minutes, the longer the better.

Meanwhile, slice the large onions into rings and, using a wide frying pan, sauté in a little oil until golden brown. Remove from the pan and set aside on a plate. These will be used for garnishing.

Leaving the same frying pan on a medium heat, lift the fillets out of the marinade and swiftly transfer to the pan. Reserve the remaining marinade. Cook covered (skin side down), for about 6 to 8 minutes, turning once. Having the lid on allows the fish to cook all over in its steam and avoids fishy cooking smells from invading the kitchen. Set aside.

The rice

In a non-stick saucepan, large enough to hold the rice and the fish, heat a little oil and sauté the finely chopped onion until golden brown. Add the stock together with two tablespoons of olive oil and whatever is left of the marinade. Add the salt and bring to the boil.

Drain the rice and tip it into the boiling stock with the chopped coriander or flat parsley. Bring to the boil again, then turn the heat down to a simmer, cover and cook for about 15 minutes.

Remove from the stove. Now, you are going to layer the dish by alternating a layer of fish with a layer of the rice.

Remove half the quantity of rice and set aside. Level the remaining rice and arrange the fish fillets evenly on top. Spread the rest of the rice on top of the fish. (Depending on the size of your pan, you may have more than two layers.)

Cover and cook on high heat for about a minute or so, then reduce the heat to a minimum and cook for another 25 minutes. It is now ready to eat, but you can pop the pan in the oven,

preheated at 100°C/gas mark ¼, and leave it there until it is time to serve.)

Serve hot garnished with onion rings.

To serve as a cake, garnish the rice with the onion rings then turn the pot upside down on a plate. (Tip: Put a plate on the top of the pot, hold it firmly down with one hand and turn the pot upside down with the other.)

Variation: This variation gives the rice a more intense flavour and the fish a sharper lemony taste. Instead of marinating the fish, you mix the marinade with the stock or water for the rice.

Sprinkle 3 tablespoons of lemon over the fish. Season with salt and pepper and marinate for 15 minutes. Heat a frying pan, lay the fish in the pan and cover. Cook on medium heat for about 5 minutes. Uncover, turn the fish over, and cook for another 4 minutes or until the water has evaporated. Set aside to cool. Then, cut up in chunks.

When you come to cook the rice, follow the recipe above and include the marinade in the water or stock. Once the rice is cooked, gently mix in the fish with the rice and cook on minimum heat for another 15 minutes. Serve hot garnished with onion rings.

Fish and rice patties

Uruq b'samak

These patties are made of fish, rice and herbs. They are then stuffed with more fish spiced up with dried lime. The large quantities of fresh coriander and parsley, mixed with the dried lime, make a heavenly combination with the fish. It is one of our most favourite dishes. Dried limes are available from most Persian or Middle Eastern shops. They should be purchased whole and ground as needed, otherwise the flavour evaporates. Cut open with a knife, take out the pips and pulverise to a fine powder in a coffee grinder or mortar and pestle.

This recipe is similar to *uruq b'ruz* (Rice patties with meat and dried lime p.25) but the taste is totally different and well worth the effort.

It is best to organise all the ingredients on your work top before starting. The preparation takes a little time but the making of the patties is easy and most enjoyable.

Makes about 18 to 20 patties

You will need, in all, 675g (1½lb) of skinned fish fillets

The stuffing
3 tablespoons oil for frying
225g haddock fillets, cubed
2 medium onions, finely chopped
¼ teaspoon cumin
½ teaspoon ground coriander
1 scant teaspoon turmeric
¼ teaspoon black pepper
7 to 8 pulverised dried limes (about 6 tablespoons)
Salt to taste

The Shell
380g rice
450g cod or haddock fillets, cubed
40g flat parsley, leaves only (or a handful)
20g fresh coriander (or ½ the amount of parsley)
1 bunch chopped spring onions (green tops only)
1 tablespoon salt

Wash the rice and drain.

Next, pulverise the dried limes. Cut open with a knife, take out the pips and pulverise to a fine powder in a coffee grinder or mortar and pestle.

Making the stuffing

Sauté the onions in 3 tablespoons of oil over a medium heat for about 2 minutes or until soft and translucent, stirring occasionally. Mix in the spices of the stuffing ingredients. Add the cubed fish and stir gently until nearly cooked. Sprinkle in the salt and the pulverised lime. Stir to mix and remove from the heat.

Making the shell

Place the fish, parsley, coriander and spring onions in a blender and make a very smooth and sticky paste, the smoother the better (remember to push down the sides of the paste and blend again).

Place the drained rice in a large bowl with one tablespoon of salt. Spoon in all fish paste. Wet your hands and mix thoroughly.

Making the patties

Prepare a bowl of cold water.

Wet your palms and take a portion of the shell mixture, the size of a large plum and gently flatten it on your palm. Place a heaped tablespoon of the filling in the centre. Keeping your hands moist, bring the sides up over the stuffing and seal. Then very gently shape it into a slightly flattened ball. Arrange on a tray and set aside.

To cook

You will be cooking the patties in two or three batches, depending on the size of your saucepan. You will be aiming to put about six to seven patties in the pan. Remember, the rice will double in size so it is important not to overcrowd them.

Half fill a wide and deep saucepan with water. Add one teaspoon turmeric, half a teaspoon salt and some pepper and bring to the boil. (This water can be used later as a clear soup to be eaten with the patties.)

Slowly lower the patties, one by one, into the boiling water making sure that all of them are submerged. Bring back to the boil, turn down the heat to a bubbling simmer and cook uncovered until they begin to float to the top – about 20 minutes. (If the heat is too high the patties might fall apart)

Remove with a slotted spoon and allow to drain before arranging on a dish.

Serving

You can **either** serve them drizzled with a little olive oil **or** in a soup bowl with a ladle or two of the cooking liquid poured over them. In keeping with tradition, you can allow them to cool and then fry them in a little oil. I like to brush them with olive oil and bake them in the oven at 200°C/Gas Mark 5 for 20 minutes or until crisp. Alternatively, as you will be cooking quite a few, you can freeze the extra ones once they have cooled down. Then, when needed, **either** steam them **or** brush them with olive oil and place in the oven without having to defrost them. They make an excellent meal, served with steamed vegetables, salad and pickles.

Barbecued fish

Masgouf

Serves 4

1.5 kg whole sea bass cut open or 850g fillets

The marinade
5 tablespoons olive oil
2 tablespoons tamarind paste or lemon juice
2 tablespoons pulverised dried lime (or 2 extra tablespoons of lemonjuice)
1 teaspoon turmeric
1 tablespoon paprika or mild curry powder
1 tablespoon salt

This is a famous Iraqi dish, made with a river fish, similar to the carp, called *shabbut*. Fishermen would bring in their catch every night on the banks of the River Tigris to sell to passers-by. The fish was cut like an open book (butterflied); then brushed with oil, seasoned with herbs and spices and skewered on wooden sticks which were planted in the ground over a brushwood fire. I remember the enticing aroma of the burning brushwood and barbecued fish, wafting up to our roof terrace where we slept during the summer months.

Masgouf used to be one of the popular dishes for parties and celebrations. Alas, it is very difficult to reproduce the taste of *masgouf* without the aromatic brushwood fire. Pan-frying, grilling or barbecuing the fish are acceptable alternatives if you marinate it with a lot of herbs and spices. If you can get a whole fish butterflied (that is to say, cut all the way down the side where the spine is), so much the better. If not, use fillets.

Combine the marinade ingredients and spread liberally over the fish. Cover and set aside in the refrigerator for about one hour.

If you are using fillets, pan-fry one side for about 5 minutes on medium heat. Carefully turn over and cook covered for another 4 minutes or so. If butterflied, similarly grill or barbecue each side until cooked.

Squeeze a little lemon juice over the fish before serving. Serve with a tomato and onion salad and some plain rice.

Vegetarian

When diet is wrong medicine is of no use.
When diet is correct medicine is of no need.

Ancient Ayurvedic Proverb

Sweet and sour aubergine with prunes

Ingryie (vegetarian)

Serves 4 to 6

3 to 4 aubergines
3 red peppers, thinly sliced
3 medium sized tomatoes,
    sliced in round discs
3 onions, thinly sliced in rings
8 pitted prunes
4 dried apricots (preferably
    the dark brown untreated
    ones)

The sauce
2 tablespoons tomato paste
2 tablespoons sugar
3 lemons, juiced
A pinch of cayenne pepper
Salt and pepper to taste

Slice the aubergine into round discs about 2cm thick. Place in a colander. Salt liberally, making sure all the slices are covered, and leave for 30 minutes.

Soak the prunes and the apricots in cold water.

Preheat the oven to 180°C/Gas Mark 4.

Next, stir-fry the onions rings, then the peppers until soft and set aside separately.

Thoroughly rinse the aubergines and pat dry with some kitchen paper. Pan-fry, on both sides, with a little olive oil. Set aside.

Lightly oil an oven dish and arrange a single layer of half the aubergine at the bottom, followed by a layer of the onions, prunes, peppers and apricots. Top this with the remaining aubergine. Finish with a layer of sliced tomatoes.

Mix all the sauce ingredients until the sugar has dissolved. It should taste a little lemony. Pour it over the vegetables and bake in the oven for about 35 minutes.

Serve hot with rice or as an accompaniment to grilled meat or fish. This dish is very tasty served cold.

Variation: Instead of frying, I grill the aubergine and pepper rings, brushed with a little olive oil. As a further variation, I sometimes like to char the skin of the peppers and remove it. This imparts a smoky flavour which I love. Removing the skin also makes for a softer texture. To do this, grill the peppers whole until the skin is black and charred; immediately pop them in a plastic bag, seal and leave them for a few minutes. This makes it very easy to peel away the charred skin.

Sweet and sour okra

Bamia hameth

Serves 4 to 5

400g frozen baby okra

The sauce
1 large onion, finely chopped
400g tomatoes, fresh or
    canned, chopped
250ml water
1 tablespoon tomato paste
2 to 3 garlic cloves, peeled
2½ lemons, juiced
A pinch of vegetable stock or
    vegetable Bouillon powder
2 tablespoons sugar or to
    taste
Salt and pepper to taste

Okra, *bamia* in Arabic, is a summer vegetable which has a very short season. My grandmothers used to thread them on a string like a necklace and dry them in the sun, to cook them in the winter or spring months when they were no longer in season. They are available frozen in Middle Eastern grocery shops and in a few supermarkets. In summer, some shops sell the fresh ones. I prefer to use the frozen ones because they are smaller and daintier and also do not require cleaning. If using fresh, remember to cook them longer.

Making the sauce

Sauté the chopped onion in the olive oil on medium heat until soft and golden. Add the tomatoes and stir to mix. Cover and simmer on a low heat for about 25 minutes, stirring occasionally. Do this until the tomatoes begin to melt. Add the tomato paste, the garlic, stock powder, water, salt and pepper, and bring to the boil. Continue a gentle boil for 5 minutes.

Add the frozen okra, bring back to the boil and turn the heat down to a simmer. Cook for about 20 to 25 minutes, depending on whether you like the okra soft or a little al dente.

Add the lemon juice and sugar and mix well. Taste and adjust the sweet and sour flavour. Simmer for another 5 to 10 minutes.

Serve hot with rice or bread.

Sweet stewed turnips

Shalgham helu

These stewed turnips with a hint of sugar are one of Baghdad's typical street foods on cold winter days. Outside our school, a street vendor used to park his cart, laden with a large pot of turnips simmering on a small kerosene stove. Their enticing aroma filled the air, attracting passers-by and pupils alike and, by lunchtime, he could hardly cope with the demand. Once cooked, these turnips look wizened and deflated but, I promise you, their taste is wonderful.

1 kg small turnips
A pinch of salt
3 tablespoons date syrup or Moscovado sugar

Wash the turnips and top and tail them. Do not peel. Place them in a large saucepan, add the salt and cold water to cover. Bring to the boil. Add the date syrup and continue boiling, covered, for 25 minutes.

Preheat the oven to 150°C/Gas Mark 2.

You **either** can continue to cook on the hob for another 30 to 40 minutes by placing a heat diffuser under the pot and reducing the heat to a simmer **or** transfer the turnips to an oven proof dish with a lid. Pour in the liquid to half cover the turnips. Bake, covered for one hour or more. The turnips will turn brown.

Serve hot and eat as a starter or part of a *mezze* spread.

Enghien es Bains – Rueil
"et pour vous satisfaire
un revente en BIO

Sweet and sour pumpkin stew

Qagh'e ahmer hameth

Serves 4

750g pumpkin or butternut
  squash, peeled and cubed
1 onion, finely chopped
1 garlic clove, finely chopped
1 piece fresh ginger 5cm long,
  finely chopped
3 heaped tablespoons
  sultanas
8 prunes, coarsely chopped
400ml tinned tomatoes,
  chopped
1 tablespoon tomato paste
3 lemons, juiced
zest of 1 orange
3 tablespoons sugar or agave
1 tablespoon olive oil
200ml water
¼ teaspoon cinnamon
1 teaspoon salt or to taste
A pinch of cayenne pepper

This traditional winter dish can also be made using butternut squash. It benefits greatly from being cooked a few hours before eating it, giving the flavours time to intensify. So I prepare it in the morning to serve it for dinner or the next day.

Gently fry the onion on a low heat until soft.

Add the garlic, ginger, cayenne pepper, cinnamon and the chopped tomatoes and turn the heat to high, stir fry for 30 seconds. Then reduce to a simmer, cover and cook for 10 minutes.

Add the water, tomato paste, sultanas, prunes, salt and sugar. Stir to mix and bring to the boil. Add the pumpkin chunks, stir to mix. Reduce the heat to medium and cook, covered, for 20 minutes. Add the lemon juice. At this point, taste and adjust the flavour of the sauce to your liking. If too lemony, add a bit more sugar and vice versa. Cover and continue to cook for another 15 minutes or until the pumpkin is tender and soft. Watch the sauce does not boil away, adding a little water if necessary.

Serve hot or cold, with white or brown *Basmati*.

Chickpea pillows

Sambusak bel tawa

Makes 35 pillows

The dough
200g self-raising flour
1 tablespoon olive oil
1 teaspoon salt
Chickpea water

The stuffing
500g chickpeas
3 or 4 large onions, finely
    chopped
125ml olive oil
2 teaspoons ground cumin
1 heaped tablespoon curry
    powder
Salt and pepper to taste

These deep fried lovelies are one of my favourite snacks and no Iraqi cook's repertoire should be without them. They are a standard offering at parties and gatherings. Traditionally, the filling is a mixture of chickpeas and chicken, but I prefer to make it with just the chickpeas. Note that the chickpeas must be soaked overnight in some lightly salted water to soften them.

Wash the chickpeas and soak overnight in some lightly salted water.

The next day, place chickpeas with their soaking water in a saucepan, cover with more water, if needed, and bring to the boil. Once boiling, reduce the heat to medium. Continue to cook, half covered, for about one hour or so. The chickpeas should be soft.

Drain and reserve the water, you will need it for the dough.

Making the dough

Mix the dough ingredients with a little of the chickpea water which will act like yeast. Wet your hands and knead into a soft paste or mix in a blender, adding more chickpea water, little by little, until you reach a malleable consistency. Cover the bowl with a plastic bag or cling film and let it rest for about 30 minutes.

Making the stuffing

Meanwhile, coarsely mash the chickpeas (you can do this in a blender or with a potato masher) and set aside.

Fry the chopped onions in the oil until golden. Reduce the heat to low and stir in the chickpea paste.

Add the curry powder and cumin, and mix well. Adjust salt and pepper to taste. Set aside.

Making the pillows

You will be cutting circles of dough of about 8cm in diameter. You can use a cookie cutter or drinking glass for this purpose.

Roll out a small quantity of the dough with a rolling pin. The dough should be thin, about 6mm thick. Cut a few circular shapes at a time, out of the dough.

Place a tablespoon of the stuffing in the middle of each circle. To ensure that the dough doesn't open while frying, dab some water on one side. Fold over the other side to make half a circle. Press down the edges firmly and set aside on a tray. Continue until you finish the dough.

You might have some stuffing left, this can be frozen and used at a later date. (You can also spread some on toasted bread with thinly sliced cucumbers on top.)

In a large pan, put enough oil to deep-fry the pillows on medium heat. It is better to fry them in batches as it gives them room to expand. Fry until crisp. Transfer on to kitchen paper to absorb any excess oil.

Variation: You can mix thin slivers of cooked chicken with the chickpea filling and proceed as above.

Pickles and preserves

These are a must in my store cupboard. I regard them as my jewels because they transform a bland ingredient or dish into something, altogether more exciting, in the same way that a beautiful brooch or necklace can dress up an otherwise simple outfit. Eaten as appetisers or as accessories to a dish, these complex exquisite tasting preserves add a sexy twist to whatever you are eating, be it plain bread, a piece of cheese, grilled meat or fish. Much as I love them, I use them with restraint, a little at a time.

In Baghdad, during the summer, women set to work making huge quantities of preserves and pickles. Ripe tomatoes would be sieved to extract their juice and pulp, then placed under the hot sun to reduce them to a paste-like consistency. This was how tomato purée was made in each household. *Bamia* (okra), threaded on a string like a necklace and left to dry in the sun, was used to make stews in the winter months when the okra was out of season. Apricots, apples, quince, figs, peaches and other fruit were made into jams, preserves or candied sweets. Small cucumbers and garlic would be pickled in brine. In winter, it was the turn of the turnip and the beetroot to be preserved in salt water and vinegar.

Although everything we ate was home made, mango pickle was not. Of course, mango pickle is Indian, but it has become a very Iraqi condiment, albeit by adoption, and used in salads, in wraps and as an accompaniment to meat or fish. I remember seeing the older pupils in my school stuffing slivers of this sunny yellow pickle into a pocket of bread called *sammoun*, and heartily munching away. It was their favourite snack. Today, in some Asian and Middle Eastern shops, one can still find the same brand that we used to buy in Baghdad, the bottle with a label showing a ship and lots of medals.

These days fruits and vegetables are available all year round spoiling us for choice. When we lived in Baghdad and Beirut, we were very aware of the changing seasons. We ate only local and seasonal produce and, therefore, preserving fruits and vegetables was our way of extending their use when they were no longer available. Sugar, salt, lemon, vinegar and sun drying were used to this end.

Pickled turnips

Mukhallala

1 kg small white turnips
4 tablespoons salt
800ml water
300ml white wine vinegar
2 raw beetroots
A bunch of flat parsley (optional)

Bring the water, vinegar and salt to the boil and stir to dissolve the salt. Take off the heat and set aside to cool.

Wash the turnips well and top and tail them; do not peel them. Make a deep slit in the shape of a cross at the top of each one. You can also quarter the turnips instead of scoring them. They will pickle a little faster.

Peel the beetroots and slice them. Pack the turnips in a pickling jar, layering the slices of beetroot in between them. These will colour the turnips bright pink.

Pour the cooled water and vinegar over the turnips covering them completely. If you are using the parsley, stuff a bunch on top and close the jar.

Keep in a warm corner of the kitchen for about ten days.

To serve, slice the pickled turnips and place in a bowl. Garnish with chopped flat parsley. You can add some more vinegar if you prefer a more sour taste. Serve with *kebab*, grilled meat or chicken and as part of a *mezze*.

Pickled olives

Zeitoun

Olives are one of the pleasures of a *mezze* table. They are also great in stews and salads or simply eaten with some Arabic bread. For the best taste, buy them from shops that sell them in large barrels of brine. If you like them bitter, choose the small green ones that have been slightly crushed and pickled with either garlic or rosemary. Ripe olives are black in colour but, that said, some of the commercially pitted ones are artificially ripened. Olives not only taste good but are, also, good for us providing us with vitamin E, copper and iron.

In south London, where we live, we have a few olive trees growing in pots on our terrace. To our surprise, these small trees started bearing fruit and so far, we have been able to pick about a kilo or two of olives every year and pickle them at home. So, should you want to pickle your own, this is how we do it:

Wash the olives and throw out any damaged ones. Put them in a plastic bag and beat them gently to crush them. Place them in a bowl of water for eight days, changing the water daily. This removes most of their bitter taste. Drain well. Place in a bowl with a few garlic cloves and a sliced chilli. Mix in the salt (about three tablespoons salt to one kilogram of olives). Leave to rest for a day and then tip them into sterilised jars and cover them with olive oil. They will be ready to eat in three weeks. You can also pickle them in brine, instead of olive oil (120g salt to 2 litres of water).

The pickling paste

Pickling paste
100g mustard
100g ground white
    pepper
50g ground black pepper
50g ground turmeric
50g sugar
50g ground ginger
50g ground coriander
50g ground cardamom
3 tablespoons salt
4 or 5 garlic cloves
About 100ml olive oil
Cider vinegar

This spicy pickling paste recipe comes from my grandmother, *Nana*. In her days she used to pickle the cucumbers first, and then immerse them in the spices for a few more days. To save time, I mix the pickling liquid with a spoonful of the pickling paste and pickle the cucumbers in one go.

This recipe is for a large quantity of pickling paste because it keeps for a long time and can be used for many pickling batches. Pickle a small batch at a time of garlic and cucumber or any other vegetable.

To make the pickling paste

It is best to grind some of these spices yourself but you can also buy them ready ground. If you are grinding, sift before putting them in a bowl with the other spices.

Heat the oil and let it cool completely. In a bowl, add the oil and the ground spices, a little at a time, and mix well. You need enough oil to make a thick paste. If the oil is too little add a little more. The paste should be stiff. Add a few pieces of garlic to the paste. Cover and leave overnight.

The next day, mix in two to three tablespoons of cider vinegar to make the paste a little thinner. Pour into a jar and leave for a week before use.

From time to time, if the paste gets too thick, add more vinegar to soften it. A little more sugar can be added, once in a while, to enhance the taste.

Pickled garlic and cucumbers
Turshi

1 kg small cucumbers or
   gherkins
5 to 6 garlic cloves, peeled
1 litre water
300ml cider vinegar
4 tablespoons salt
1 heaped tablespoon of
   pickling paste

Bring the water, vinegar and salt to the boil and stir to dissolve the salt. Take off the heat and set aside to cool. Once the liquid has cooled down a little, stir in one heaped tablespoon of the pickling paste. Set aside.

Wash the cucumbers, dry them and make a small slit at one end.

Pack them in a pickling jar with the garlic cloves.

Pour in the pickling liquid, covering them. Close tightly and keep for 10 days or more before consuming. The longer the better.

Preserved lemons in lemon juice

8 unwaxed lemons
12 tablespoons salt
Lemon juice to fill your jar

Scrub the lemons thoroughly. Cut them each into eight pieces, discarding the pips. Place them in a bowl and sprinkle them with the salt. Mix well and set aside for a few hours. Pack them in a sterilised jar (they should fill the jar completely) and close.

Leave in a cool dark place for three days and then pour in the lemon juice to the brim. Seal with a little olive oil at the top. This stops them from moulding. Close the jar and keep for about three weeks, when they will be ready to eat.

I use these lemons for cooking in stews. If you want to eat them as an appetiser or a side dish, I recommend putting them in a dish steeped in olive oil to soften the sour taste, or, better still, use the following recipe, Preserved lemons 'express', instead.

Preserved lemons 'express'

8 unwaxed lemons
12 tablespoons of salt
3 cloves garlic
2 chillies cut lengthways

Heat the oven to 200°C/Gas Mark 6.

Scrub the lemons thoroughly and lightly score the skin in four places from top to bottom.

Arrange them in an ovenproof dish with some water to half cover them. Pop them in the oven and bake for about 45 minutes.

Remove from the oven and let them cool down a little. Cut each one into eight pieces, picking out all the pips. Place them in a bowl and sprinkle all over with the salt. Let them rest for an hour.

Pack them, with their juice, in a sterilised jar, layering the garlic and chillies in between the lemons. Fill the jar with olive oil, covering the lemons completely. They will be ready to eat in five days. Keep the oil – it is wonderfully fragrant in salad dressings.

Variation: Instead of putting them in the oven, you can boil them in a large saucepan full of water for about 20 minutes. Let them cool down a little and then proceed as above.

Serve at the same time as the *turshi pickles* (p.161), and the *mukhallala (p.158)* or use in salads or with steamed fish.

Green Tomato Chutney

This is a delicious chutney that will excite your palate. We grow our own tomatoes in London and at the end of each summer we end up with bagfuls of green ones which will not mature any more. This recipe has come to our rescue and we make a sweet and spicy relish out of them. You can make this chutney with red tomatoes too.

1 kg green tomatoes, finely chopped
3 garlic cloves, chopped
A long piece of root ginger, 10cm long, finely chopped
2 pieces of crystallised ginger, chopped
5 red chillies
250g apples, peeled, cored and finely chopped
220g shallots or onions, finely chopped
80g raisins, chopped
1 tablespoon salt
190g unrefined cane sugar or *Moscovado* sugar
200ml malt or cider vinegar

Place all the ingredients in a saucepan and bring to the boil. Keep stirring so that the sugar dissolves completely. Do this for a few minutes and then simmer, gently, for an hour and a half. Take off the heat. Using a blender, roughly blitz the mixture to make a smoother and thicker consistency. Allow to cool and pour into a sterilised jar. Cover and place in the fridge.

Serve with grilled meat or fish or, on its own, on fresh bread.

Sweets, Desserts and Jams

Although I do not have a sweet tooth, I have chosen some very sweet specialities because, apart from being visually appealing, their distinctive and delicate flavour of rosewater, cardamom, almonds and pistachios, are wonderfully evocative – sending me straight back to my childhood and to my Baghdadi community.

When I eat one of these, it is not the sweetness that I taste first, but the flavour of belonging.

Baklava
Baklawa

All the countries of the Middle East make this famous dessert and all call it their own. Characterised by the fine layering of dough, interspaced with nuts and honey, *baklava*'s precise origin is unknown. However, earliest records show that the Assyrians, around 8th C BCE, were sandwiching honey and nuts between crude layers of flat dough. We also know that this was improved, much later, by the Greeks who made a similar but lighter dish, thanks to their invention of the *'filo'* pastry. The dough, rolled out as thin as a leaf and almost transparent, was named *filo*, meaning leaf. This delicate pastry improved the sweet considerably.

Over the centuries, Baklava was further refined as it spread from Greece to Turkey, to Persia and the Caucasus. It reached its height under the Ottomans who were very interested in food and perfected many dishes. They called this sweet dessert *'Baqlagu'* from where, it is believed, Baklava derives its name. As a result the whole Middle East adopted it and made it for special occasions, such as a marriage or an engagement as well as religious feasts.

Today, each country makes it in a slightly different way; some cut it into lozenges, others into squares, some make the portions large, others make them very small and delicate, some put almonds only, others pistachios and almonds, and so on. In Iraq, rosewater is added to the nuts and syrup, giving it a delicately perfumed taste.

Baklava
Baqlawa

Baklava is a sandwich of very fine layers of filo pastry, interspersed with nuts and drowned in syrup. Filo pastry has to be handled with great care as it tears easily. It must be covered to stay moist because it dries up quickly. There are many brands of filo; some are frozen and need to be totally defrosted before use, others are ready to use. Follow the manufacturer's instructions before starting this recipe.

> 450g filo pastry
> 380g unsalted butter
>
> **The filling**
> 650g almonds
> 2 tablespoons sugar
> 1 tablespoon ground cardamom
> 2 tablespoons rosewater
>
> **The syrup**
> 675 sugar
> 420ml water
> 2 tablespoons lemon juice
> 2 tablespoons rosewater

Making the syrup

Combine the sugar, lemon juice, and water in a saucepan and simmer over low heat to dissolve the sugar. Stir and continue simmering until the liquid thickens. Stir in the rosewater. Remove from the heat and set aside to cool.

Pre-heat the oven to 180°C/Gas Mark 4.

Making the filling

Blanch the almonds in boiling water and grind coarsely. Mix the ground almonds, sugar, cardamom and rosewater in a bowl.

Making the *baklava*

Cut the whole stack of filo pastry the size of your the baking tray. (Cover with cling film or a damp cloth while assembling.) Lightly grease the baking tray.

Melt the butter on an extremely low heat. (You can use a double boiler for this). Do not burn.

Place a sheet of filo, one at a time, in the tray and brush every second sheet with the melted butter. Once you have laid four sheets, spread some of the nut mixture over the pastry. Lay another four sheets of filo on top, brushing every second one with butter. Now, spread the rest of the nuts on top and cover with six sheets of filo, brushing every second one with butter.

Using a sharp knife, cut the pastry all the way to the bottom layer, in four or five equidistant straight lines. Cut again diagonally, to make small diamond shaped portions. (You can also cut the *baklava* into small squares).

If you have some butter left, pour it over the whole pastry. Place in the oven and bake for 20 minutes. Reduce the temperature to 150°C and bake for another 20 minutes or until golden brown. Remove from the oven and pour the cooled syrup over it. It is up to you how much syrup you want to use.

Let it cool down completely before serving although I find it tastier when eaten the next day.

Variation: Pistachios can be used instead of almonds or a mixture of walnuts and almonds.

Almonds

Loz

An almond, picked and eaten straight from the tree, has a soft texture and a delicate, milky taste. If you have not experienced eating fresh almonds before and you cannot obtain them, I suggest you do the following: place some almonds in a bowl of water (just enough to cover them) and leave them to soak overnight. By morning they will have become soft and taste very similar to the fresh ones.

We are very fond of almonds in the Middle East. We eat them fresh, roasted or coated with sugar and include them in most of our sweet pastries. Rich in fibre and vitamin E, almonds constitute a good source of calcium. They bring a delicate and distinctive flavour when used in cakes, puddings and pastries or when added to *pilau* rice and stews.

It is a good idea to store the almonds in an airtight container and preferably, in a cool place or in the refrigerator as over time their monounsaturated oil could turn and become rancid. I do this with most nuts and seeds.

My mother's almond macaroons
Hadji bada

Special almond macaroons, deliciously chewy with a hint of rosewater, are traditionally made for the Passover feast. They are so popular with everyone that we make them these days, all year round. We call them *hadji bada*. My mother's recipe makes an interestingly different macaroon; rough textured as opposed to smooth, a favourite of mine.

500g blanched almonds, coarsely ground
320g sugar
The whites of 3 medium eggs, lightly beaten
1 heaped teaspoon ground cardamom
Rosewater

Pre-heat the oven to 170°C/Gas Mark 3. Have a bowl with a little rosewater in it, for wetting your hands.

In a bowl, mix the almonds, sugar and cardamom. Add the egg whites and knead into a malleable dough. Cover and leave to rest in the refrigerator for a few hours or overnight if you wish.

Line a baking tray with greaseproof or baking paper. Lightly wet your hands with the rosewater and take a little of the dough the size of a walnut and shape it into a tight ball, flattening the top a little with your finger. Arrange on a tray, spacing the balls to avoid them sticking to each other as they expand when baked. Bake for about 15 to 20 minutes or until golden.

Leave to cool completely before handling. Serve or store in an airtight container in the refrigerator or freezer where they will keep well for a long time.

Variation: My Aunt Eileen makes these traditionally smooth textured macaroons. They contain walnuts as well as almonds, double the amount of eggs and are deliciously chewy.

> **500g blanched almonds, finely ground**
> **200g walnuts, finely ground**
> **500g caster sugar**
> **1 teaspoon ground cardamom**
> **The whites of 5 medium eggs**
> **1 egg yolk**
> **Rosewater**

Pre-heat the oven to 160°C/Gas Mark 2. Have a bowl with a little rosewater in it, for wetting your hands. In a bowl, mix the almonds, walnuts, sugar and cardamom. Add the egg whites and the egg yolk, then knead into a malleable dough, and continue as above.

Almond cigars with rosewater
Malfouf

Malfouf is an Arabic word meaning 'wrapped'. This sweet snack of almonds, wrapped in filo pastry, is a speciality of the Babylonian Jewish community. It is served with tea or coffee, after a meal or when friends come to visit. The combination of almonds, cardamom and rosewater is heavenly.

Filo pastry is paper thin – almost as fragile as gold leaf! From the Greek word meaning leaf, filo has to be handled with great care as it tears easily. It must be covered to stay moist because it dries up quickly. There are many brands of filo; some are frozen and need to be totally defrosted before use, others are ready to use. Just follow the instructions on the packet.

Before starting this recipe, have two clean tea towels ready as follows:

One to cover the unused sheets of filo pastry.

One very slightly damp, to cover the cigars while waiting to go in the oven.

Makes about 50 pieces

450g filo pastry
225g blanched almonds, coarsely ground
45g of sugar
4 teaspoons ground cardamom
3 teaspoons rosewater

Preheat the oven to 180°C/Gas Mark 4.

Combine the ground almonds, sugar and cardamom in a bowl. Mix well and stir in the rosewater.

Carefully lay out a sheet of filo pastry on your work top. Cut the sheet into three long strips about 10cm wide.

Take one strip and place a round stick about 5cm from the edge. (You can use a round chopstick or the round handle of a wooden spoon; just make sure it is not too thick as this will determine the thickness of the cigar.) Fold the filo over the handle and arrange a spoonful of the mixture along the fold line, leaving about 1cm free at either end. Roll the pastry to the end, then squeeze both ends towards each other to crinkle the cigar. Slip out the handle and crimp both ends.

Arrange the *malfouf* in the baking tray as close together as possible. This will stop them unfolding. Cook for 10 to 15 minutes. You want the pastry to be crisp but not toasted.

Allow to cool completely before handling.

Aromatic almond milk pudding

Muhallabi

A Middle Eastern favourite, this deliciously fragrant pudding is traditionally made with full fat milk. Some people add cream as well to make it very rich. I use almond milk instead because members of my family are lactose intolerant. Happily, the almond milk enhances the flavour even further, making the pudding light and aromatic. You can make it with milk, if you prefer.

Serves 4 to 6

1 litre almond milk (with no added sugar, if possible)
7 tablespoons cornflour
5 tablespoons sugar
2 whole cardamom pods
2 teaspoons vanilla essence
2½ tablespoons rosewater

For the garnish
1 tablespoon finely ground cardamom pods
1 tablespoon pistachios, coarsely ground

Mix the cornflour with a little almond milk into a smooth paste. Set aside.

Place a saucepan over medium heat. Combine the rest of the almond milk with the sugar and cardamom pods and slowly bring to the boil, stirring frequently.

Remove from the heat and pick out the cardamom pods. Add the cornflour paste and blend in well. Return to a low heat, stirring constantly until the mixture thickens (this will take about 10 to 15 minutes). Be careful not to let the mixture stick to the bottom of the pan.

Remove from the heat and add the rosewater. Give it a good stir. Pour into individual dishes or a large bowl and garnish with a sprinkling of pistachios and ground cardamom. Set aside to cool, then cover and place in the refrigerator for 15 minutes or more. Serve chilled.

Dates

Tamer

The date palm, or the 'nakhla' as it is called in Arabic, has always been regarded as the 'Tree of Life'; the staple food for those living in the desert, providing them with food and shelter from the burning sun.

The *nakhla* is one of the oldest fruit trees in the world. Archaeological evidence shows that it was cultivated thousands of years ago and as early as 4000 BCE in ancient Mesopotamia. The date palm is indigenous to southern Iraq, Arabia and the Persian Gulf area, although its exact origin is not known. It remains a very important crop in the Middle East and North Africa, and until five years ago Iraq was the world's biggest producer and exporter of dates, followed by Saudi Arabia. This ancient fruit is also cultivated in California and in the arid deserts of Israel.

As well as providing food, its branches and leaves are used for building and roofing materials; for making baskets, mats and rope; and from its sap, sugar is made. It is also invaluable for the shade it provides.

Dates are rich in glucose and fructose as well as potassium, vitamin A and B-complex. They are eaten raw, stuffed with nuts or dipped in *tahina*. They add a sweet note to stews, puddings and pastries. They are also processed into a thick syrup, called *dibis*, which we use as a jam or in cooking instead of sugar.

Date cookies

B'ab'e b'tamer

These are savoury biscuits, filled with meltingly soft date centres, and usually served to guests as a snack with tea or coffee, along with cheese *sambousaks* and *malfouf.*

The dough

This is a basic recipe for dough which you can use for making savoury or sweet snacks. I find plain flour works successfully with the yoghurt. You can add a teaspoon of baking powder to this if you wish or use self-raising instead of plain flour.

Making the dough

Sieve the flour, fennel and salt into a mixing bowl. Add the butter, cut and rub in. Add the yoghurt and mix. Knead into a malleable dough. (Add some water, if needed). Cover with a damp cloth and leave for about an hour in a warm part of the kitchen.

Making the filling

Combine the dates with the butter and oil in a saucepan and place on a very low heat. Stir with a fork for about five minutes or until the dates become malleable. Add two or three tablespoons of water to get a smooth paste. Set aside to cool.

Once the paste is cool enough to handle, grease the palm of your hands with a little oil and roll a heaped teaspoonful of the mixture into a ball. Do this with all the date mixture and place the balls on a plate.

Makes about 45 cookies

500g plain flour
140g butter (room temperature)
150g yoghurt (room temperature)
1 flat teaspoon salt
1 teaspoons ground fennel
Some lukewarm water

The filling
500g soft pitted dates
15g unsalted butter (room temperature or softer)
1 tablespoon sunflower oil
3 tablespoons water

1 egg yolk, beaten (for glazing)
Some sesame seeds

Making the cookies

Pre-heat the oven to 180°C/Gas Mark 4.

You will be cutting circles of dough of about 8cm in diameter. You can use a cookie cutter or drinking glass for this purpose. Knead the dough for a few minutes. Take a small portion at a time and roll out with a rolling pin. The dough should be thin, about 6mm thick. Cut as many circular shapes as you can. Gently gather up the leftover dough and set aside in a covered bowl.

Place a date ball in the centre of each circle. Gently gather up the edges of the dough to cover the filling. Press the edges firmly together to seal and gently flatten it with the palm of your hand.

Turn the cookie over and roll lightly with a rolling pin to flatten it further. Do not press too hard otherwise the filling will ooze out. I like these very thin, so experiment until you find the right pressure to use.

Repeat until the leftover dough and filling have been used.

Arrange the cookies on a baking tray. Using a fork, prick the surface several times to stop the cookies from puffing up. Brush them lightly with the egg, then sprinkle a few sesame seeds on top. Bake in the preheated oven for about 30 minutes or until golden.

Serve warm or cold.

If you have some dough left it can be kept in the refrigerator or frozen, as long as you wrap it in cling film or foil. You can safely mix it later with a new batch of dough.

Nutty date balls
Madgooga

There are a few variations of this recipe. This is my friend Vivian's recipe which she makes to perfection. The pecan nuts give it a wonderfully distinctive taste. A word of warning though, once you eat one of these date balls you will not be able to stop.

200g almonds, coarsely chopped
200g dried dates, pitted and finely chopped
100g walnuts, coarsely chopped
100g pecan nuts, coarsely chopped
75g brown cane sugar
75g white granulated sugar
5 egg whites, beaten with a fork until fluffy with bubbles

Pre-heat the oven to 160°C/Gas Mark 3.

Combine all the ingredients and leave to stand for about 30 minutes. Mix again and, with wet hands, take a small portion and roll into a walnut-sized ball. Do this until you use up the mixture. Place on a baking tray lined with grease proof or baking paper. Bake for about 15 to 20 minutes or until golden brown.

If some are out of shape adjust them while they are still hot and malleable, but otherwise leave to cool down completely before handling them any further. They can be frozen and eaten at a later date.

Cheese Pillows

Sambousak b'jeben

These *sambousaks* are one of my favourite savoury finger foods. A speciality of the Babylonian Jewish community, they are made for home consumption, celebrations, parties, or served to guests at teatime. Usually a large number of these *sambousaks* are made up in one go, some of which are then frozen and reheated when needed. You might be wondering why I have included a savoury recipe in the dessert section. The dough composition is the same as the recipe for the date cookies. For practical reasons the two recipes are usually prepared at the same time. It is always more fun to be two when making these. So choose a day when you can bake together with a friend.

Makes about 60 pillows

The dough

I find plain flour works successfully with the yoghurt. You can add a teaspoon of baking powder if you wish or use self raising instead of plain flour.

500g plain flour
140g butter (room temperature)
150g yoghurt (room temperature)
1 level teaspoon salt
1 teaspoons ground fennel
Some lukewarm water

The Filling
1 egg
500g grated white cheese (A mixture of cheddar cheese and *haloumi* works well)

For glazing (optional)
1 beaten egg and some sesame seeds

Making the dough

Sieve the flour, fennel and salt into a mixing bowl. Add the butter and cut and rub in. Add the yoghurt and mix. Knead into a malleable dough. (Add some water, if needed.) Cover with a damp cloth and leave for about an hour in a warm part of the kitchen.

Making the filling

Beat the egg and the cheese together in a bowl and set aside.

Making the *sambousaks*

Pre-heat the oven to 180°C/Gas Mark 4.

You will be cutting circles of dough of about 8cm in diameter. You can use a cookie cutter or drinking glass for this purpose. Knead the dough for a few minutes. Take a small portion at a time and roll out with a rolling pin. The dough should be thin, about 6mm thick. Cut out as many circular shapes as you can. Gently gather up the leftover dough and set aside in a covered bowl.

Place a heaped teaspoon of the filling in the middle of each circle. To ensure that the dough doesn't open while baking, with the tip of your finger dab some water on one side. Fold over the other side to make half a circle. Press down the edges firmly and set aside.

Repeat until the dough and stuffing have been used.

Arrange the *sambousaks* on a tray lined with greaseproof or baking paper. Lightly brush the tops with the beaten egg yolk. Bake for about 25 minutes or until golden. Serve warm or cold.

If you have some dough left it can be kept in the refrigerator or frozen, as long as you wrap it in cling film or foil. You can safely mix it later with a new batch of dough.

Candied orange peel
Qshour pourtaqal

You can use any citrus fruit peel to make these delicious candied rings. My Aunt Eileen makes the best ones that I have tasted. Below is her recipe. A friend of mine asked me what I did with the oranges once the peel has been taken off. In fact, it is the other way round. Before eating an orange I wash and grate it lightly, score it into eight equal parts, peel it and freeze the skins. Once I have collected a sufficient amount, I make the recipe.

> 6 large oranges
> 500g sugar
> 1 tablespoon lemon juice
>   (or 1 teaspoon citric acid)

Lightly grate the surface of each orange. You only want to take off the tiniest amount.

Score the skin into eight equal parts and peel away each segment.

Place the peel in a large pot and generously cover with water. Bring to the boil and continue boiling, uncovered, for five minutes.

Drain and discard the water. Return to the pot and cover with cold water again. Bring to the boil and continue boiling, uncovered, for a further five minutes. Drain and leave to cool.

These two stages remove the bitterness.

Roll each peel into a curl and insert a toothpick to secure. Repeat until all the strips are rolled.

Rinse the pot so as to remove any bitter residue.

Pour the sugar and 700ml water into the pot and bring to the boil. Put in all the rolled peel. Make sure the water covers the peel; if not, add some more. Continue boiling, uncovered, until the syrup reduces to half.

Now drizzle in the lemon juice (or citric acid) and keep boiling until the syrup reduces to a thick liquid, covering about half a centimetre at the bottom of the pot. You will be basting the peel with it.

Remove from the heat and tilt the saucepan to one side to allow the syrup to flow out. Spoon the syrup, many times over the peel. Pull out each toothpick holding down the roll with a fork so that it does not unravel. Transfer to a plate and leave to cool completely.

Put the candied peel in the refrigerator, uncovered, for 24 hours before serving or freezing.

(You can roll them in dessicated coconut, after taking the toothpicks out. Any leftover syrup can be used as jam.)

Apple jam
Murabbat tiffah

The addition of rosewater and cardamom makes this jam wonderfully aromatic. It is my mother's recipe, which she makes for *Rosh Hashana,* the Jewish New Year. You can use Golden Delicious or Royal Gala apples.

1 kg apples, peeled, cored, seeded and quartered
1 lemon, juiced
730g sugar
7 whole cardamom pods
1 tablespoon rosewater
200ml water

Combine the sugar with the water in a large saucepan. Simmer on medium heat, stirring until the sugar dissolves. Add the apples, rosewater, cardamom and lemon juice. Bring back to the boil, then turn down to a low simmer and cook, covered, for 2½ hours or until the apples are soft and the syrup is very thick.

Allow to cool completely before transferring to airtight jars. Store in the refrigerator. Serve with soft cheese or *tahina* and bread or toast.

Apricot preserve

Marabat mishmish

1 kg of fresh apricots (firm and not too ripe)
450g sugar
2 tablespoons lemon juice

Wash and slice the apricots in half and remove the stones.

In a suitably sized pot, combine the sugar and apricots, mixing well. I find that arranging the apricots and sugar in layers makes it easier to mix. Cover and set aside overnight at room temperature. This releases the apricot juices so that no water need be added.

The next day bring the pot to the boil. Reduce the heat to a gentle simmer, add the lemon juice and cover. Do not stir or mix. Cook for one hour, gently shaking the pot from time to time to mix the fruit with the syrup. This will soften the apricot halves without loss of shape, but you can adjust your cooking time to suit the required consistency.

Let the preserve cool completely before pouring into a sterilized jar.

Halva ice cream

This dessert is quite rich but so exquisite that it is worth making, even if you have to limit yourself to eating one or two spoonfuls.

Vanilla ice cream or non-dairy ice cream
Plain halva

Let the ice cream soften a little, but do not defrost. Blend the halva with the ice cream. Mix well. Put in a cake mould and freeze. Serve as a cake.

Drinks

We should look for someone to eat and drink with before looking for something to eat and drink.

Epicurus

Teas and infusions

The following infusions are not only refreshing and soothing, many have properties that ease digestive and respiratory problems.

Dried lime tea *Chye noomi Basra*

This lemony tea has a lovely smoky taste. It is also a well tried potion which stops a runny tummy efficiently. You can add honey if you like.

Break up two or three dried limes into a saucepan. Add some water and bring to the boil. Reduce the heat, cover and simmer gently for 10 minutes.

Pour into a teapot, add more boiling water if needed and serve.

Cumin tea *Chye kummoon*

The health benefits of this spice have been known since ancient times. Apart from aiding digestion and reducing flatulence, it has beneficial effects on the respiratory system. It is also known for its detoxifying properties, its trace minerals and high iron content.

Put one teaspoon of cumin seeds in a pan with some water. Bring to the boil and immediately reduce the heat. Cover and simmer gently for 10 minutes. Set aside to rest for 5 minutes. Serve strained.

Fennel tea *Chye habbet helwah*

High in vitamin C, potassium and dietary fibre, fennel has a light but distinctive taste similar to liquorice. Its seeds are often eaten raw after a meal to cleanse one's breath or to help reduce bloating and other digestive complaints.

Lightly crush one or two teaspoons of fennel seeds in a pestle and mortar and place in a saucepan (you can also put them whole, the taste will be less strong). Add some hot water and simmer for 10 minutes. Do not boil. Serve strained. You can add honey, but the fennel flavour is so delicate it is best to drink it neat.

Fresh mint tea *Chye na'na*

Mint is an important ingredient in Iraqi and Middle Eastern cooking and has many health benefits. Rich in vitamin A and C, mint is used for relieving heartburn, to soothe stomach cramps and other digestive discomforts. The antiseptic properties of peppermint oil, when inhaled, helps clear colds and the respiratory tract. It is a refreshing drink at any time of the day.

Wash about 15 to 20 fresh mint leaves and drop them in a tea pot. Pour hot, but not boiling, water over them and steep for about 5 to 10 minutes. Drink as is or with some honey.

Dried raisin juice *Qeddous*

I use organic raisins because they come without any vegetable oil on them. Most commercial products are oiled to prevent the raisins from sticking. This sweet drink was made for the Friday night meal by my grandmother as a substitute for wine.

500g raisins

Wash the raisins and tip them into a large bowl or saucepan and cover completely with water. The raisins will expand so the water needs to be about 5cm or so above them. Cover and leave overnight. The next day, strain the liquid and set aside. Put the raisins back in the bowl and pour in a little water. Set aside for a few hours. Strain the liquid through a very fine strainer and add it to the first raisin water. Place in the refrigerator. Serve cold.

Variation: You can also boil the raisins for about 30 minutes. Allow to cool and sieve through a muslin squeezing out all the juice.

Serve chilled.

Hot almond drink

H'riri

I think this is the most delicious and delectable drink of all time. Traditionally, we have it once a year to break the fast of Yom Kippur. After a 25 hour fast, the first thing we put in our hungry stomachs is this soothing, very creamy, almond nectar. Some people add rosewater and cardamom but my preference is to only taste the delicate flavour of the almonds.

It is easy to prepare and makes a change from drinking coffee or tea.

Serves 10 cups

800g whole almonds, soaked overnight
2½ litres water
8 to 9 tablespoons sugar
1 large cheesecloth or muslin

Finely grind the almonds with four tablespoons of water in a blender.

Place one and a half litre of water in a deep pot and the other litre in a bowl.

Place the ground almonds in the centre of the cheesecloth (if using muslin, which is thinner, fold it over once) and close the sides. Tie tightly with a rubber band or string so as to make a sack.

Immerse the sack in the water of the pot and squeeze it to draw out the milk. Squeeze for about 10 to 15 minutes or until you have squeezed most of the milk out. Then place the sack of almonds in the bowl water and squeeze some more. This will produce more milk.

When you are satisfied that you have squeezed all the milk out, combine this water with that in the pot, add the sugar and stir well to mix. Bring to the boil, then simmer gently, uncovered, for about 25 minutes, stirring occasionally. The longer you simmer the thicker the milk becomes.

Serve hot in cups or mugs, using a soup ladle.

Note: Do not throw away the milked ground almonds. You can make a wonderfully light cake out of them. Mix the ground almonds with 2 medium eggs, 2 tablespoons of wholemeal flour, 1 teaspoon baking powder, 80g sugar and 1 teaspoon vanilla essence. Spread on a baking tray (about 40 by 30cm) lined with a non-stick paper or Teflon sheet. Bake in a preheated oven 180°C/Gas Mark 4 for 20 minutes or until the top becomes dark brown. Turn over to toast the other side for 10 minutes, (you might have to cut it in half to do this). Cut into strips and let it cool before serving.

Yoghurt sherbet
Shenina

We call it *shenina*, the Indians call it *lassi* and the Persians call it *doogh*. This drink is so refreshing on a hot summer's day.

Fill a third of a glass with your favourite yoghurt, add water and a pinch of salt and mix well. You may put in an ice cube or two.

Rosewater Sherbet
My Warid

An exotic and perfumed drink to quench your summer thirst.

Fill a glass with water. Add one teaspoon of distilled rosewater and half a teaspoon of sugar and mix well. Serve with an ice cube or two.

Alternatively, you can make a drink called *Café Blanc* by adding the rosewater to a cup of hot water, sweetened with a little sugar if desired. Some people drink this instead of coffee at the end of a meal.

Orange blossom sherbet
My qeddah

Fill a glass with water. Add a teaspoon of distilled orange blossom and half a teaspoon of sugar. Mix well and serve with an ice cube or two. You can also make *café blanc* as above.

Tea

Chaye

Those who did not own a samovar made a makeshift one by imitating its principle. After filling the tea pot with tea leaves and hot water, it was placed on top of a kettle of boiling water (with no lid) which was simmering gently on the stove. Brewing thus for a long time, it provided hot strong tea all day long. The tea was sipped black from a small glass called *istikan*, mixed with plenty of sugar and sometimes, with a cardamom pod. The Persian way is to put a cube of crystallised sugar in one's mouth rather than in the glass and drink the tea through it. This tea is always drunk black, with hot water added to taste. You could try popping a cardamom pod or two in the teapot.

Coffee
Qahwa

Arabic coffee

The coffee houses in Baghdad served an incredibly strong coffee, called *qahwa murra,* to its male clients who sat talking or playing backgammon. Simmered for a long time to evaporate most of its water, the coffee became a concentrated bitter brew, of which only a few drops at a time were poured in to the miniature coffee cups. For obvious reasons it is always served with a glass of water.

Turkish coffee
Qahwa turkia

Most of us love this less intense coffee. Always black, with or without sugar, Turkish coffee is served in small cups after a meal, or at parties where the women have fun 'reading' the future from the sediment at the bottom of the cups. Most people like to lift the flavour by adding a pod of cardamom.

Serves 4

4½ **coffee cups of water**
4 **teaspoons of very finely ground coffee**
   (it should have the consistency of talcum powder)
3 **to 4 whole cardamom pods**
2 **teaspoons sugar or to taste (optional)**

Put the coffee, cardamom, and the water in a saucepan and bring slowly to the boil. The minute it starts boiling remove from the heat, skim off the froth and put a little of it in each cup. Return to the stove, and gently bring to the boil again. Turn off the heat, skim off some more froth, add to the coffee cups, and pour in the coffee. The froth will rise to the top.

Other recipes

Inspired by my travels
and my Middle Eastern background

In this second part of the book you will find recipes that I have adopted, adapted or created. The accent here is on light and easy to prepare dishes which have a touch of the East. My love of fish pushes me to discover and invent different ways of marinating and cooking it. I use it in various salads and as a main ingredient in the recipes that follow.

The success of your dish depends, first and foremost, on the freshness and provenance of your ingredients. Equally, as I have already mentioned, recipes are not set in stone; they can be altered to suit your taste. So always taste as you cook and be brave in adjusting the seasoning and spices.

Cucumber rolls with soft goat cheese

This is my modern take on the Middle Eastern salad of cucumbers, yoghurt and garlic. Very refreshing and visually pleasing, it makes a delightful starter.

Serves 2

100g very soft goat cheese or cream cheese
1 cucumber (small Mediterranean one, if possible)
Extra virgin olive oil to mix
A pinch of *za'atar*
Salt and cayenne pepper to taste
½ a clove garlic, finely minced or crushed
1 fresh tomato, diced (for garnish)

Wash the cucumber. Do not peel. With a potato peeler, slice the cucumbers lengthwise into paper thin strips and lay them flat on a chopping board.

Mix the goat cheese with two tablespoons of olive oil or more to make a smooth paste. Add the cayenne pepper, the salt and the garlic and mix well. Put a teaspoon of the mixture at one end of the cucumber strips and roll carefully to the end. Do this with as many strips as you need.

To prepare individual servings, drizzle a little olive oil on each plate and arrange upright with four or five rolls per person. Decorate with the chopped tomato and sprinkle liberally with *za'atar*. You can drizzle on some more olive oil if you wish.

Variation: Another starter, this serves one of the above cucumber rolls for each person. Put two tablespoons of yoghurt in the middle of each individual plate. Pour two tablespoons of olive oil over it. Season with salt and pepper. Then stand the roll in the middle of the yoghurt. Arrange a few cucumber slices all around the plate and decorate with the chopped tomatoes. Sprinkle generously with *za'atar*.

Serve with warm wholemeal pitta bread.

Aubergine salads

The buttery texture and smoky flavour of the charred aubergine give a truly distinctive taste to the salads below.

Serves 2

1 large aubergine
½ a lemon, juiced
1 fresh tomato, finely chopped
2 tablespoons extra virgin olive oil
½ teaspoon *sumac* (optional)
½ teaspoon cayenne pepper (optional)
Salt and pepper to taste
**1 tablespoon each of finely chopped
    spring onions and parsley to garnish**

Wash the aubergine and prick it all over with a fork. This will stop it from bursting while being charred or grilled.

Char grill the skin of the whole aubergine directly on the fire of the hob until it turns black. You can do this under the grill too, it will take a little longer about 40 minutes.

Allow to cool sufficiently to peel off the skin and top and tail it. The inside should be quite soft.

Place on a plate and cut into cubes of approximately two centimetres.

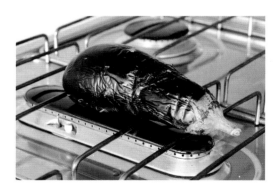

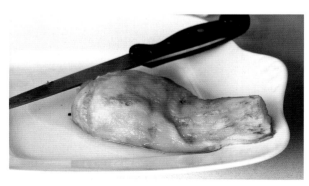

Arrange the aubergine on a serving dish.

Combine the lemon juice, tomatoes, olive oil, salt and pepper, and drizzle over the aubergine. Sprinkle with *sumac* and cayenne pepper if using. Garnish with the spring onions and chopped parsley.

Variation 1: This is exactly the same recipe with an addition of 150g thick goat's yoghurt and an extra tablespoon of olive oil added to the dressing. Pour over the cubed aubergine. Garnish as above.

Variation 2: This version has a different dressing which includes *tahina* (sesame paste). The taste is amazing.

Serves 1 or 2

1 aubergine charred and cut into cubes.

The Dressing
3 tablespoons *tahina*
4 tablespoons lemon juice
4 tablespoons water
3 tablespoons extra virgin olive oil
4 tablespoons yoghurt
½ teaspoon salt or to taste
½ teaspoon cayenne pepper or to taste
Pepper to taste

Mix the dressing ingredients into a creamy paste.

Pour the dressing on top of the warm aubergine.

Warm potato salad with turmeric

Serves 4

4 potatoes
2 tablespoons lemon juice
5 tablespoons extra virgin olive oil
½ garlic clove, crushed
½ teaspoon turmeric
½ teaspoon cayenne pepper
1 teaspoon salt or to taste
A handful of flat parsley, finely chopped
2 spring onions, finely chopped

For this salad choose potatoes that are floury and can better absorb the dressing.

Wash and peel the potatoes and cut them into bite-sized chunks. Steam for 10 minutes or until they are cooked. Do not overcook them as they will disintegrate in the salad.

In the meantime, mix the crushed garlic with the salt in a salad bowl. Add the lemon juice, turmeric and the cayenne pepper. Mix well. Stir in the olive oil.

Transfer the hot potatoes into the salad bowl and mix gently. When the potatoes are hot they quickly absorb the dressing. Taste and adjust by putting more lemon juice or olive oil or salt.

Garnish with the spring onions and the parsley.

Serve warm or at room temperature.

Puy lentils and grapefruit salad

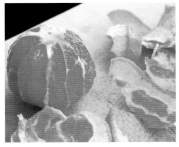

500g Puy lentils
2 grapefruits

The dressing
1 tablespoon lemon juice
1 grapefruit, juiced
2 tablespoons extra virgin olive oil
2 tablespoons chopped fresh coriander
A sprinkling of cumin (optional)
Salt and pepper to taste

Wash the lentils and cook, half covered, on medium heat for 25 minutes or until the lentils are cooked. Puy lentils will always feel a little firmer than the ordinary green ones.

Cut away the peel and the pith of the grapefruits. With a sharp knife cut out the segments and set aside.

Drain the lentils and set aside in a salad bowl to cool.

Mix the dressing ingredients. Combine the lentils and grapefruit segments. Pour the dressing and toss to mix. Garnish with the chopped coriander.

Refrigerate for 15 minutes and serve chilled rather than very cold.

Samphire

I discovered samphire some 25 years ago when I was living in Paris.
My local fishmonger used to sell it during the month of July and August.
Intrigued, I bought a handful one day and used it in a salad with some ripe
tomatoes. Ever since I have become a fan of this maritime plant. Named
Saint Pierre in French, after the patron saint of fishermen, samphire is a
hardy, succulent, bright green plant which grows on tidal marshes and on
rocks by the sea. Norfolk is a good place to pick your own, at low tide.
I use it raw in salads because of its crunchy texture, or lightly steamed and
serve it as a vegetable. Be careful not to sprinkle any additional salt to
your dishes when using it, as it is very salty. You can buy samphire from
good fishmongers and supermarkets.

**2 handfuls of samphire (choose the more delicate
and less woody ones)
2 fresh tomatoes, coarsely chopped
1 spring onion
1 tablespoon lemon juice
2 to 3 tablespoons extra virgin olive oil**

Wash the samphire, combine with the tomatoes in a bowl. Drizzle the
lemon juice and olive oil on top and mix. Serve with grilled or steamed fish.

Avocado

Avocado is one of my all time favourite fruits. The word 'avocado' has its root in the Aztec word *'ahucatl'*, meaning testicle – a reference to its shape – which can be like a pear or spherical. The Aztecs also regarded the *'ahucatl'* as a fertility fruit and an enhancer of sexual potency. Also known as butter pear or alligator pear, avocados were originally native to Mexico and parts of South America. They are grown worldwide today.

Like bananas, avocados mature on the tree but ripen off it. Once picked, they should be put in a warm place to allow them to ripen successfully. They will not ripen in the refrigerator. When cut open and exposed to the air they will oxidise and go brown. To avoid this, dip them in a little lemon juice.

The avocado is versatile and very nourishing. It is rich in minerals and vitamins and has the highest protein and fat content of any fruit. Because its fat is monounsaturated, a diet rich in avocados has been shown to lower the bad cholesterol and increase the good one. It can be eaten as a dessert with a sprinkling of sugar as they do in Brazil, or as a savoury ingredient in salads, sushi and in dips such as guacamole.

Layered spinach avocado and tomato salad

Spinach leaves (baby or the
   mature type)
1 ripe avocado
1 ripe fresh tomato
2 lemons, juiced (in a bowl for
   the avocado)

The Dressing
1 tablespoon lemon juice
3 tablespoons extra virgin
   olive oil
½ teaspoon salt
A pinch of cayenne pepper
1 garlic clove

This warm, layered salad makes a fabulous starter. You will need cooking rings of 10cm in diameter (as individual portions), which you can easily find in the kitchen section of a department store. For this recipe I have not put the exact amount of each ingredient, as this is difficult to measure in this case. Suffice it to say you need a small amount of everything!

Making the dressing

Crush the garlic clove with the salt in a small bowl. Add the lemon juice and the cayenne and mix. Add the olive oil, mix again and set aside.

Cut the avocado in half, remove the stone and peel off the skin. Slice thinly across the width and put the slices in the bowl of lemon juice and mix well, making sure that all slices are coated.

Slice the tomatoes thinly in rings and set aside.

Wash the spinach and steam in a covered pan for about 4 to 5 minutes or until it begins to wilt. Set aside.

Making the portions

Place a cooking ring in the middle of the plate and pour in one tablespoon of olive oil. Take some warm spinach leaves and arrange a layer inside the ring. They should take up half the height of the ring. Sprinkle with salt and drizzle with another tablespoon of olive oil. Layer the avocado slices on top of the spinach. You can make one layer or two, depending on how thin your slices are. Sprinkle some salt and a tablespoon of lemon juice over the top.

Arrange the tomatoes over the avocado and pour 1 tablespoon of the dressing over it.

Just before serving remove the ring carefully. You can garnish with some parsley if you wish.

Mixed leaf salad with avocado and orange

I sometimes make this salad using just rocket leaves or in combination with romaine lettuce and baby spinach leaves. Both versions work well. If you have some preserved lemons, finely chop half a lemon and include it with its oil in the dressing. The taste will be more intense.

Serves 4

2 ripe avocados
2 oranges, peeled and segmented
1 spring onion, finely chopped
2 large handfuls of mixed leaves
   (lettuce, spinach, wild rocket, etc)
3 tablespoons of lemon juice
6 tablespoons extra virgin olive oil
   (or a combination of olive and hemp oil)
Flat parsley, finely chopped
½ teaspoon salt or to taste
A pinch or two of cayenne pepper

Combine the lemon juice, salt and cayenne pepper in a salad bowl.

Cut the avocados in half, remove the stones and peel off the skin. Slice thinly across the width and put the slices in the salad bowl with the lemon juice; mix well making sure that all slices are coated.

Peel the oranges, taking off all the white pith, and with a very sharp knife, cut out the orange segments. Do this carefully so as not to break them, and set aside.

Now, mix in the spring onions and the segments of orange in the bowl with the avocados. Pour over the oil and mix gently.

Lay the mixed leaves and parsley on top. Mix the salad just before serving. This will ensure that the leaves stay crisp.

Linda's spicy summer salad

Ever since I first made this salad twenty years ago it has been a favourite with all my friends and family. The combination of the buttery avocados and the cod is out of this world.

Serves 6

600g thick cod fillets, skinned
2 to 3 ripe avocados
3 lemons, juiced
   (in a bowl for the avocado)
2 spring onions, finely chopped
A few rocket leaves, flat parsley
   and chilli flakes for the garnish

The Dressing

2 lemons, juiced
6 to 7 tablespoons of
   extra virgin olive oil
½ teaspoon salt and
   pepper to taste

Wash the fish fillets and pat dry with a paper towel. Season with salt and pepper. Steam them for about 10 minutes or until cooked. Transfer the cooked fish on to a flat plate and set aside to cool down completely. Sprinkle with some lemon juice and a pinch of salt.

Put the juice of 3 lemons and the spring onions in a bowl. Season with a little salt. Cut the avocado in half, remove the stone and peel off the skin. Slice thinly across the width and put the slices in the bowl of lemon juice; mix well, making sure that all slices are coated.

When the fish has cooled down, you can use your hands to divide it into segments. This is how the fish is structured and these segments come away easily. In a large platter, arrange the fish and avocado alternately. Pour the rest of the lemon juice over the salad.

Combine the dressing ingredients, mix well and pour over the salad. Sprinkle with cayenne pepper or chilli flakes. Finish off with a garnish of rocket leaves and parsley. Chill in the refrigerator and serve cold.

Variation: This salad works well with baked beetroots in place of the fish.

Warm haddock and mung beans salad with olives

This is another salad using fish. Delicious, healthy and easy to rustle up.

Serves 2

300g haddock fillets, skinned
150g mung beans, soaked overnight
A handful of flat parsley, coarsely chopped
1 lemon, juiced
5 tablespoons extra virgin olive oil
A few black olives
Salt and pepper to taste
¼ teaspoon cayenne pepper

Wash the beans and soak overnight.

Drain and cook the beans in boiling water for about 15 to 20 minutes or until tender. Do not overcook, as the beans will become mushy in the salad.

Wash the fish fillets and pat dry with a paper towel. Season with salt and pepper. Steam them for about 10 minutes or until cooked.

Carefully transfer the cooked fish on to a flat plate and set aside.

Drain the cooked beans and place in a salad bowl. Flake the fish and lay it on top of the beans. Do not mix or stir at this point. Sprinkle with salt and pepper, pour in the lemon juice followed by the olive oil and mix gently.

Scatter the olives and flat parsley on top and serve warm with some bread.

Linda's wild salad

Serves 4

250g Canadian wild rice
550g wild salmon fillets
2 spring onion stalks, finely
    sliced
1 small shallot, sliced into rings
1 orange, for the zest and
    flesh
1 orange for the juice
6 tablespoons sweet
    pomegranate seeds
6 to 7 tablespoons finely
    chopped fresh coriander

The marinade
1 lemon, juiced
1 shallot, grated
1 teaspoon agave or honey
A pinch of cayenne pepper
Salt and pepper to taste

The dressing
3 tablespoons lemon juice
5 tablespoons orange juice
5 tablespoons extra virgin
    olive oil
1 teaspoon agave or honey
A pinch of cayenne pepper
Salt and pepper to taste

The vivid orange colours of the wild salmon, the ruby red pomegranate seeds, and the emerald green coriander leaves on the dark brown, almost black, backdrop of wild rice is a visual treat. The taste is sublime too!

Wash the rice and drain. Tip into a saucepan with a lot of water and bring to the boil. Lower the heat and simmer for 55 minutes, or follow the directions on the packet.

Meanwhile, mix the marinade ingredients in a bowl. Cut the fish into small portions and combine with the marinade. Place in the refrigerator for 30 minutes.

Wash the orange. Lightly grate off the zest and set aside. Cut away the peel and the pith with a very sharp knife. Gently cut out the segments and set aside.

Heat a frying pan on medium-low heat, without any oil. Put in the fish, cover and cook for about 7 to 8 minutes, turning once. Set aside.

Drain the rice and tip into a large salad bowl. Mix in the spring onions and arrange the fish and the orange segments on top. Sprinkle with the coriander, orange zest, shallot rings and the pomegranate seeds. Pour the dressing and toss lightly to mix. Adjust the taste and seasoning.

Serve warm. Wild rice hardens when cold, so tip any leftover salad with its dressing into a pan and heat before serving.

Variation: Brown quinoa can be used instead of the wild rice.

Courgette and carrot tagliatelli

I remember wanting to do something exciting with the one carrot and one courgette that remained in my fridge. I did not want to chop them and put them in a soup. I wanted something different. The result is this very light, warm and moist salad. Packed with subtle flavours, it only takes a few minutes to cook.

Serves 1 or 2

1 carrot
1 courgette
1 tablespoon lemon juice
1 tablespoon extra virgin olive oil
Salt to taste

Wash the carrot and the courgette and peel.

Using a good peeler preferably with a moveable blade, peel the carrot and courgette into paper-thin strips.

Transfer the strips into a saucepan with 3 tablespoons of water. Cover tightly and turn up the heat to high for 15 seconds. Then turn down to the lowest setting and cook for about 10 to 12 minutes or until the strips have wilted. It is best to use a diffuser for this as the heat needs to be at a minimum. You can lift the lid after 8 minutes, fluff up the strips and check if they are done; if not, cover quickly again, and cook for a few more minutes. The vegetables should steam in their own juice.

Gently lift the strips with a fork, and place in a salad bowl. Sprinkle a pinch of salt and pour on the lemon juice and olive oil. Toss lightly. The salad should feel moist.

Serve warm.

Quinoa

I was thrilled when I discovered this grain-like seed 12 years ago – it was love at first bite! I loved its nutty taste and its crunchy texture.

Not only is quinoa delicious and versatile (I cook it often to replace rice or *burghul* wheat or to make various salads) it is also amazingly nutritious and beneficial to our immune system. High in protein (deemed complete as it includes all nine essential amino-acids) quinoa also provides fibre and a host of minerals and vitamins.

Cultivated over thousands of years ago in the high mountains of South America, it was the staple food of the indigenous population of that region. It was so valued by the Incas that they called this super seed the 'mother seed', on a par with gold.

Quinoa seeds can be black, brownish red or white, and are easy to cook, very much like rice. You must rinse the seeds thoroughly to take off the bitter natural coating found on its husk. To achieve a nuttier taste, dry roast the washed seeds in a saucepan until they dry completely and then tip them into boiling water.

Simple quinoa

This is served hot or cold as an alternative to rice, couscous or *burghul* wheat, to accompany various stews and salads.

Serves 2 to 4

300g brown or white quinoa
Salt and pepper to taste
Extra virgin olive oil

Rinse the quinoa seeds a few times, then dry roast them in a saucepan, on low heat, stirring occasionally, until they are completely dry. This should take about four minutes.

Cover with twice its volume of water, add salt and pepper, and bring to the boil. Reduce the heat to a low simmer and cook covered for about 15 to 20 minutes, or until the tiny white spirals appear. Be careful not to overcook the quinoa or you will end up with a mushy porridge.

Drain and serve hot with a drizzle of olive oil.

Variation: Add a chopped onion, a whole garlic clove and some organic vegetable or chicken stock in the boiling water, then add the quinoa.

Brown quinoa salad with pomegranate seeds

This is a flavoursome and healthy salad, with an interesting crunchy texture. As with the simple quinoa, be careful not to overcook.

Serves 4 to 6

250g brown quinoa
2 spring onion stalks, finely chopped
The seeds of 3 pomegranates
1 orange, juiced
1 lemon, juiced
4 to 5 fresh cherry tomatoes, halved or quartered
4 to 5 tablespoons of extra virgin olive oil
Salt and pepper to taste

Rinse the quinoa seeds a few times, then dry roast them in a saucepan, on low heat, stirring occasionally, until they are completely dry. This should take about 4 minutes.

Cover with twice its volume of water, add salt and pepper, and bring to the boil. Reduce the heat to a low simmer and cook covered for about 15 to 20 minutes, or until the tiny white spirals appear.

Drain and transfer to a salad bowl and allow to cool down, fluffing it every so often with a fork.

Add the spring onions, the pomegranate seeds, salt and pepper, the lemon, orange juice and olive oil, and mix gently with two forks. Taste and adjust the seasoning.

Garnish with the tomatoes and flat parsley.

Chicken stew with preserved lemons and olives

Serves 4 to 6

1 whole chicken (about 1.5 kg)
1 tablespoon ground ginger
½ teaspoon ground cinnamon
1 to 1½ teaspoons ground
    turmeric
3cm fresh ginger, finely
    chopped
1 to 2 cloves garlic, crushed

2 to 3 tablespoons olive oil
1 medium onion, finely
    chopped

About 550ml water or chicken
    stock
20 green or black whole
    olives, pitted
2 to 3 preserved lemons,
    quartered (p.162)
4 tablespoons fresh coriander,
    coarsely chopped
4 tablespoons flat leaf
    parsley, coarsely chopped
Salt and pepper to taste

I have adapted this famous Moroccan dish to suit my family's taste buds by adding some fresh ginger and using turmeric instead of saffron. The combination of the chicken and preserved lemon is truly delicious. If you do not have preserved lemon, you can add lemon and lemon zest instead. Of course, the taste will be different.

Skin the chicken and remove as much of the fat as you can, together with the parson's nose. Wash the whole chicken and pat dry. Rub the chicken inside and out with a piece of cut lemon. This helps to clean it and remove any unpleasant odours. Joint into eight to ten pieces.

Combine the ground and fresh ginger, the cinnamon, the turmeric and the garlic, with a pinch of salt, and crush well to mix into a paste. Set aside.

Heat the oil in a heavy-bottomed pot, add the onion and fry gently until soft and golden brown. Turn the heat down to a simmer and stir in the spice paste. Cook until the aroma rises. This should take a few seconds. Lay in the chicken pieces, followed by the preserved lemons and olives, and mix well. Cover and simmer for about 15 minutes or until the liquid has almost evaporated.

Add the 550ml water or stock, salt and pepper to taste, stir to mix and bring to the boil. When adding salt, bear in mind that the preserved lemons are very salty. Then sprinkle in the chopped coriander and parsley. Continue to simmer covered for 1 to 1½ hours or until the chicken is very tender.

Garnish with some chopped parsley and coriander leaves.

I usually serve this dish with turmeric rice.

Marinated chicken with ginger and soy sauce

Serves 4 to 6

1 chicken (about 1.5 kg) or chicken pieces
2 tablespoons vegetable oil
A piece of ginger 3cm long, finely chopped
1 onion finely chopped
A pinch of salt and pepper
600ml of water or vegetable stock

The marinade:
2 tablespoons of cider vinegar
A piece of ginger 3cm long, crushed
3 garlic cloves
1½ tablespoon light soy sauce
½ tablespoon dark soy sauce

Wash the chicken, cut into 8 to 10 pieces and remove the skin and fat.

Mix the marinade ingredients and pour over the chicken. Set aside for half an hour.

In a saucepan, fry the onion and ginger in the vegetable oil until golden and fragrant. Add the chicken with its marinade, and stir. Cook covered on low heat for 10 minutes. Then, add the water and continue simmering on low heat for about an hour or until the chicken is tender.

Serve hot with white rice.

Marinated chicken livers

This makes a delicious quick snack or light meal. You can buy organic chicken livers in packs from reputable supermarkets. I used to love eating liver soft and pink in the middle, but I no longer consider that to be safe, so I cook it thoroughly.

Serves 2 to 3

500g organic chicken livers
3 tablespoons lemon juice

The marinade
1 clove garlic, crushed
2 tablespoons olive oil
2 tablespoons soy sauce
Pepper to taste

Mix the marinade ingredients in a bowl. Add the livers and mix well. Place in the refrigerator for 20 minutes or more.

Using a wide saucepan, pour in the marinade with the livers, cover, and simmer gently for about 8 minutes, or until well done. Drizzle with the lemon juice. Serve hot with mashed sweet potatoes.

Variation: Serve cold, sliced in a salad of avocado, spring onions and chopped tomatoes, with lots of chopped flat parsley. Drizzle some lemon juice and olive oil on top and mix.

Fish

Fish is one of the quickest foods to cook and yet many people are reticent about cooking it for various reasons: too smelly, too afraid to handle it and, of course, because they do not like the taste. A fish recipe can be very simple or very elaborate. It is up to you to choose what suits your taste. If cooked simply, it is deliciously versatile.

I usually steam it and dress it up with preserved lemons or with some chutney. I like to serve it with a mash of celeriac, carrots or potatoes. I love fish in salads too, spiced up with chillies, some coriander or flat parsley, lime juice and, of course, olive oil. Fish and lime are a marriage made in heaven.

When steaming fish, whether whole or filleted, I place it on a heatproof plate and put the plate in a steamer or on the metal grill of my wok, leaving a little space around the edges for the steam to rise. This is so as not to lose any of its precious juices. I then pour some boiling water into the steamer or wok and cover and cook on high heat for about 10 to 15 minutes, depending on the size of the fish. It is important not to put too much water as it might rise and cover the fish when boiling.

Simply steamed haddock

Serves 2

400g haddock fillet (or any other white fish)
1 fresh tomato, sliced in rings
2 spring onions, coarsely chopped
1 preserved lemon, coarsely chopped
1 lemon, juiced
Olive oil
Salt and pepper to taste
A pinch or two of cayenne pepper

Cut the fillets into individual portions.

Arrange on an oven-proof plate that will fit in your steamer or on the metal grill of your wok. Arrange the tomatoes and spring onions on top. Cover and bring to the boil. Steam for about 8 minutes. When the flesh becomes opaque the fish is cooked.

Arrange on a serving dish with some pickled lemon. Drizzle some olive oil and the lemon juice on top. Season with a pinch of cayenne pepper, or salt and pepper, to taste. Garnish with chopped fresh coriander or parsley.

Serve with a purée of celeriac and sweet potato.

Variation: You can use fillets or a whole fish.

Cut thin slices of one large tomato and one onion. Place them on a large sheet of aluminium foil. Lay the fish on top. Sprinkle with a tablespoon of lemon or lime juice, and a tablespoon of olive oil. Season with salt and pepper. Garnish with chopped coriander, chopped fresh ginger and sliced red chillies.

Close the foil by scrunching the ends only, making a big envelope out of the sheet. Place in a preheated oven to 180°C/Gas Mark 4. Bake for about 20 to 25 minutes or more depending on the size of your fish.

Fish stew in white wine and preserved lemons

In many of our Iraqi recipes we cook the fish with dried limes, coriander and turmeric. I have kept the combination for this recipe substituting the lime with the preserved lemons. In addition, I have included a dry white wine in the sauce. The flavours truly sing out.

Serves 4

600g skinned fish fillets (a mixture of salmon
   and haddock)

The marinade
1 tablespoon crushed fresh root ginger
½ tablespoon cayenne pepper
1 teaspoon ground turmeric
2 tablespoons lemon juice
5 tablespoons finely chopped fresh coriander
Salt and pepper to taste
2 tablespoons olive oil

The sauce
1 tablespoon olive oil
1 onion, very finely chopped
1 teaspoon ground turmeric
A pinch cayenne pepper
½ preserved lemon, very finely chopped
3 tablespoons finely chopped fresh coriander
150ml dry white wine
200ml water
1 teaspoon vegetable stock or vegetable Bouillon
   powder (optional)

Cut the fish into small chunks.

In a bowl, combine the marinade ingredients with the fish, which should be well coated. Cover and set aside for about an hour or so in the refrigerator.

To make the sauce, heat the oil in a saucepan (large or wide enough to accommodate the fish in one layer) and sauté the onions until soft and golden. Add the preserved lemon and stir fry for a minute or two. Add the ground turmeric and the 200ml water, and bring to the boil.

Turn down the heat and simmer, covered, for about 15 minutes, or until the lemon peel is soft. As the liquid starts to dry out, add some more hot water, about 150ml and continue simmering until the liquid reduces to a more concentrated, slightly sticky, sauce.

Stir in the white wine and the chopped coriander. Arrange the fish in the sauce and spoon the sauce over the pieces. Cover and bring to the boil, then immediately reduce the heat to low and simmer for about 6 to 7 minutes, or until the fish turns opaque. Do not stir to mix, as this will break up the fish, but shake the saucepan, from time to time .

Serve hot with rice or a potato and celeriac purée. Enjoy a glass of dry white wine with your dish.

Leftovers are delicious eaten cold, the next day. Combine them with a warm sweet potato purée, drizzled with some lemon juice and olive oil.

Variation: If you do not have the preserved lemons, substitute 4 tablespoons of lemon zest in the marinade and add a little more wine.

Cod with ginger and soy sauce

Serves 6

1 kg cod fillets or any other firm white fish
5cm cube fresh ginger, peeled and thinly sliced
2 big bunches of spring onions, shredded
100 to 150ml soy sauce, or to taste
120ml sunflower oil

Cut the fish into individual portions.

Arrange on an oven-proof plate that will fit in your steamer or on the metal grill of your wok. Sprinkle the sliced ginger on top of each portion. Bring to the boil, then cover and turn down the heat to medium. Steam for about 8 minutes. When the flesh becomes opaque the fish is cooked.

Gently arrange the fish on a serving dish, cover with the spring onion and set aside.

Heat the sunflower oil on a high heat until it begins to smoke, then immediately pour it over the spring onions and fish. The spring onions will wilt. Drizzle the soy sauce over the top. Then tilt the dish towards you, scoop up the sauce with a spoon and baste the fish.

Serve immediately with plain boiled or steamed rice.

The fish is also tasty the next day when eaten cold.

Coco fish
Marinated fish in coconut milk

1 kg skinned cod or haddock
    fillets
1 small onion, finely chopped
1 clove garlic, finely chopped
3cm cube of fresh ginger,
    peeled and finely chopped
Zest of 2 limes
400g (1 tin) coconut milk
½ teaspoon turmeric
2 red chillies, thinly sliced
    lengthways
7 kaffir lime leaves
4 small fresh tomatoes,
    quartered for garnish

The marinade
1 large lemon or two small
    lemons, juiced
1 small onion, finely chopped
½ teaspoon ground turmeric
Salt and pepper to taste

This is an easy and wonderfully fragrant recipe, adapted from one I heard on a travel program. We cook it quite often and have named it Coco Fish. Don't be put off by the number of ingredients, which consist mostly of spices.

Cut the fish into individual portions.

In a bowl, combine the marinade ingredients with the fish and coat well. Cover and set aside for about an hour or so in the refrigerator.

Fry the garlic, ginger and onion, for one minute on medium heat or as soon as the garlic begins to colour. (A wok is ideal for this purpose.) Add the lime zest and the coconut milk and stir to mix. Add the turmeric and stir again. Then, add the chillies and the kaffir lime leaves. Cook for a further five minutes, continuing to stir the sauce.

Turn the heat down to a simmer and gently lower in the fish portions with the marinade. Cook, uncovered, for about 10 minutes.

Add the quartered tomatoes and simmer for another half minute.

Serve immediately with steamed or boiled white rice. (You can cook this dish in advance and warm it very gently before serving.)

Tinned sardines

I have never looked down on the humble sardine and my store cupboard always contains a few tins. Named after the Italian island of Sardinia, where lots of them were first discovered, there is nothing like them for a quick snack when time is short. Requiring almost no preparation, they are versatile and one of the most nutritious fast foods available. Packed with a concentrated amount of vitamin A and D, omega-3, vitamin B12 and calcium, these small oily fish are very good for you, whether fresh or in tins.

They can be eaten with tomatoes and onions, with boiled or mashed potatoes, stuffed in a warm pitta with lots of flat parsley, olives and spring onions, or eaten on their own with a sprinkling of lemon juice or balsamic vinegar and cayenne pepper.

I prefer the ones in olive oil or brine. You may want to rinse them before eating them, to wash off the excess salt or oil.

Variation: I sometimes substitute tinned mackerel which provide the same health benefits.

Quickest pasta dish

You can rustle up this punchy spicy dish in less than ten minutes. The recipe works best with fresh, thin spaghettini or linguini, as these are lighter and more delicate than the hard wheat pasta. If you do not have the fresh ones try it with the usual dry pasta, it tastes good too. I use thick goat's yoghurt because I love the taste. That said, you can use the yoghurt of your choice, as long as it is thick.

Serves 2

300g fresh spaghettini or thin linguini
200g goat's yoghurt
3 cloves garlic, crushed
1 teaspoon salt
5 tablespoons olive oil
2 tablespoons coarsely chopped flat parsley
¼ teaspoon cayenne pepper

Make the sauce first as the pasta will only take two to three minutes to cook.

Put the crushed garlic and the salt in a serving bowl and mix. Blend in the olive oil, add the yoghurt and mix well.

Put the fresh pasta in the boiling water and cook, following the instructions on the packet – usually three minutes. Drain and tip the pasta into the serving bowl and mix thoroughly with the sauce.

Add the flat parsley, sprinkle a good dose of cayenne pepper and toss. *Et voilà!*

Serve hot as a starter.

Variation: You can add a few olives and two to three anchovy fillets, roughly chopped, to the yoghurt sauce.

Pasta in mushroom sauce

You can use any fresh pasta. I prefer fresh fine linguini or ravioli stuffed with spinach and cheese which you can buy in most supermarkets.

Serves 4

500g fresh pasta or ravioli
500g chestnut mushrooms
3 onions, finely chopped
250ml milk or soya milk
1 heaped teaspoon salt
½ teaspoon cayenne pepper (or to taste)
5 tablespoons olive oil
Parmesan cheese

Heat 2 tablespoons of the olive oil in a large pan and add the chopped onions. Allow five minutes on high heat, stirring continuously. Turn down to a simmer, cover and cook for about 30 minutes, stirring every now and again, until the onions become brown and caramelised.

Whilst the onions are simmering, wash and slice the mushrooms, then add them to the caramelised onions. Mix well, turn the heat to high and cook for a few more minutes, stirring continuously.

Turn the heat down to a simmer. Cover and cook for a further 25 minutes or until the mushroom juices have evaporated. Uncover and cook for a further 5 minutes stirring occasionally.

Add the heaped teaspoon of salt (or less if you prefer, but remember this is the only salt seasoning for the whole dish). Add some cayenne pepper (I usually put half a teaspoon), and stir to mix. Remove from the heat and add the soya milk and the remaining olive oil. Stir to mix and set aside.

Cook the pasta in boiling water, following the directions on the packet. Drain and tip into a serving bowl. Pour the mushroom sauce over it and mix well. Sprinkle with parmesan cheese and serve immediately.

Baked plums in their own syrup

This is a wonderfully healthy dessert and so easy to make.

1 kg red plums
Yoghurt

Preheat the oven to 200°C/Gas Mark 6.

Wash the plums thoroughly and place in a large oven-proof dish. Bake covered for an hour or until the plums have melted and their juices have oozed out.

Allow to cool and place in the refrigerator. (When cold, the juices thicken to a honey-like consistency.)

Serve cold with a spoonful or two of thick yoghurt.

An empty belly is the best cook

Estonian Proverb

Spiced baked apples

1 kg of apples, peeled, cored and quartered.
  (Bramley apples or Golden Delicious.)
3 teaspoons ground cinnamon
¼ teaspoon ground cloves
½ teaspoon ground cardamom
Vanilla ice cream

Preheat the oven to 200°C/Gas Mark 6.

Combine all the ingredients in an oven-proof dish and mix together until the apples are covered with the spices. Bake covered for about 30 minutes or until the apples have melted.

Serve warm with a ball of vanilla ice cream.

My spiced tea

6 crushed cardamom pods
3 whole cloves
4cm cube fresh ginger, crushed or grated
1 teaspoon ground cinnamon
½ teaspoon whole fennel seeds
½ teaspoon cayenne pepper
1 tablespoon honey
1 sachet camomile or fennel tea

Combine all the ingredients in a saucepan. Pour a little boiling water over them. Mix and bring to the boil and then simmer gently for 10 minutes. Pour the lot into a teapot. Fill the pot with boiling water. Stir in the honey until it melts. Drop in the sachet of camomile or fennel. Leave to brew for 5 minutes and serve.

Variation: You can put the spices straight into in a teapot and fill it with boiling water. This will make a lighter and less intense brew.

Instant coffee ice cream dessert

I do not drink coffee usually, but I love it in this dessert.

Put 4 heaped teaspoons of instant coffee in a mug. Pour in about four to five tablespoons of boiling water. Mix the water with the coffee. Do not put too much water, as the coffee needs to be very strong.

Put two scoops of vanilla ice cream in four individual bowls and spoon some of the coffee over them.

Serve immediately with a thin biscuit.

Acknowledgements

This book could not have been complete without the generous assistance and hands-on participation and talent of so many wonderful people!

My thanks and gratitude are due first and foremost to my mother for showing me, at an early age, the beauty and magic of cooking; for giving me her invaluable advice, sharing her know-how and spending time during these last two years trying out many new recipes.

My thanks go to my Aunt Doreen for being an enthusiastic follower of this project and for sharing with me her tips and cooking experiences, especially on *mahasha* and *kubba*.

For proof reading the manuscript and providing me with her recipes, guidance and suggestions; for the numerous telephone calls and emails she was subjected to during the last two years, my gratitude and special thanks are due to my Aunt Eileen.

I am indebted to my dear friend Jennifer Joseph for her invaluable IT help and for making time, *in extremis*, to painstakingly proof read and edit with me the final manuscript of this book.

My warmest thanks are to the following for their creative input, and enthusiastic support: Lucy Astor, Samantha Ellis, my nephews Jesse and Reuben Dangoor, Yvonne Saltoon, Judy and David Dangoor, Freddy Khalastchi, Hilda Aaronson, Evette Shamash, Lisette Keats, Megan Cook, Zenaida Dumaraos and my two sisters-in-law, Eve and Vickie Khalastchi; Sonia Shalam for her energy and creative ideas, Amanda Ellis for experimenting and cooking with me, Gracie Rushty for organising a lively baking session at her home, Aurora Borbon for her dedication and help in the kitchen, and all the other women that I might have, inadvertently and unintentionally, forgotten to mention.

I would like to thank my father, Abdulla Dangoor, for his constructive comments, whilst I read bits of the manuscript to him; Mike and Elwyn Blacker and Cindy Edler of Blacker Design for their professional help and expertise. A warm thank you to Claudia Roden for taking time off from her busy schedule to write her thoughts on my book.

Finally, my warmest and special thanks are to my husband, Frank, for his characteristic patience; for being my audience whenever I wanted to run a new chapter by him and, most importantly, for his unceasing encouragement and support during all the times I thought of giving up.

This project has been a journey of discovery and a reaffirmation of my roots. Above all, it has been filled with conviviality and friendship, rooted in the love of food.

Selected Bibliography

AMIR, E. *The Dove Flyer*, Halban Publishers 2009

BENJAMIN, M. *Last Days in Babylon*, Bloomsbury Publishing 2008

ERASMUS, U. *Fats that Heal Fats that Kill*, Alive Books 1993

GILBERT, M. *In Ishmael's House*, Yale University Press 2010

INY, D. *The Best of Baghdad Cooking*, E.P.Dutton 1977

KATTAN, N. *Farewell Babylon* Raincoast Books 2005

MORAD, T. *Iraq's Last Jews*, Palgrave

REJWAN, N. *The last Jews in Baghdad*, University of Texas Press 2004

REJWAN, N. *The Jews of Iraq*, Weidenfeld Nicholson 1985

RODEN, C. *The Book of Jewish Food* Penguin Books 1997

SHASHOU, A. *Alice's International Cuisine*, Summerfield Press 1992

TANNAHILL, R. *Food in History*, Three Rivers Press 1989

The SCRIBE, *The Journal of the Babylonian Jews*,
    http//www.thescribe.com

VISSER, M. *Much Depends on Dinner*, Penguin Books 1989

VISSER, M. *The Rituals of Dinner*, Penguin Books 1991

YAHIA, M. *When the Grey Beetles Took over Baghdad*, Peter Halban
    Publishers 2000

INDEX

Recipe for Contentment

Take roots of praise and thanksgiving and herbs of trust and joy, removing from them all seeds of misery and anxiety. Now take blossoms from pomegranates of knowledge and understanding and some roots of patience and contentment. Pound all these in a bowl made of humility and boil in a pan of modesty.

Add some sweetness of the lips and mix thoroughly, basting the mixture with the juice of grace and kindness.

Give two spoonfuls each morning and night to a sufferer from despair, adding three further spoonfuls of reason and communication, making sure that these are entirely free of any residue formed by bad temper and anger.

Add further a grain of acceptance of God's will, and give the patient to drink out of a vessel formed by God's praises. The sufferer will then find rest and tranquillity. Whoever follows this prescription will perfect himself and heal his soul, and he will prosper in all his ways and in all that he does.

Maimonides (1135–1204)